Understanding Differentiation

A Teacher's Guide

Sylvia McNamara and Gill Moreton

David Fulton Publishers

London

David Fulton Publishers Ltd
Ormond House, 26–27 Boswell Street, London WC1N 3JD

First published in Great Britain by David Fulton Publishers 1997
Reprinted 1998

British Library Cataloguing in Publication Data
A catalogue record for this book is available from the British Library

ISBN 1–85346–457–0

Typeset by Sheila Knight
Printed in Great Britain by Bell and Bain Ltd, Glasgow

Contents

Chapter 1

A Model for Differentiation

The ideas in this book are not new. The understanding about how children learn has been identified and discussed in many other books as a result of teachers and researchers observing children. What we seek to do in this book is to help teachers understand how these insights about children's learning translate into planning for differentiation. With this purpose we have developed a model for differentiation that has its foundation in the following: Vygotsky's theory of thought and language; Hart's (1996) collaborative learning; Bruner's ideas (1983, 1985, 1986) on scaffolding; Rogers' (1961) and Egan's (1982) work on skills training for counselling and effective communication in pairs; Seligman's (1978) learned helplessness; Craske's (1988) research on attribution retraining, and Pramling's (1988) work sharing criteria for success with children; Gipps' work (1995) on assessment and learning as separate activities; Coopersmith's (1967) and Burns' (1982) theory of self esteem and academic success; Topping's (1988) research on the benefits of peer tutoring, and Gardner's (1993) thoughts on children's learning styles.

Whilst these theories have had a profound influence on researchers in the field of education, to the authors' disappointment we have seen little evidence that the theories have impacted on classroom practice. In order to help teachers to understand and apply these theories we seek both to explain the theories and to demonstrate their relevance to the issue of differentiation. In so doing we have developed a model which combines the effective use of co-operation and collaboration, peer tutoring, group structures that promote talk for learning and open-ended investigations which offer choice in recording their outcomes. This model provides a way of differentiating the curriculum to mixed ability classes whilst supporting children's independence as learners and enhancing their self-esteem.

The teachers with whom we have worked tell us they recognise that children have different abilities and that they understand the need to differentiate in order to accommodate these different abilities. However, many of these teachers feel overwhelmed and frustrated at the amount of work and relative lack of success they have experienced as a result of struggling to differentiate. For most teachers differentiation is about differentiating the task itself and matching the task to the child's ability. What many teachers may not have considered is that they need to differentiate not because of different abilities but because children learn in different ways. The view informing the approach taken in this book is that the effects of differentiating the task are often negative so it may be more appropriate to provide choice about how the task is done in order for children to learn in their preferred way. The strategies we offer derive from our belief about the way most children learn most effectively. That is, through talk and collaboration and support.

This book sets out to provide teachers with a model of differentiation and with ways in which the various parts of that model can be adapted to teach the core and foundation subjects of the National Curriculum. It focuses on the skills training that children need so that they can be successful and independent in their learning. It is a model which does away with the dependency that Differentiation by Task often creates. It challenges the notion that differentiation is about accepting different standards and end points from children depending on their ability and argues that this form of Differentiation by Outcome creates low teacher expectations of children. It equally rejects the notion that in order to get all children to the same end point we need to teach them all in exactly the same way. The model sees the current interpretation of the debate about teaching styles as overly simplistic and unhelpfully polarised between child-centred liberals

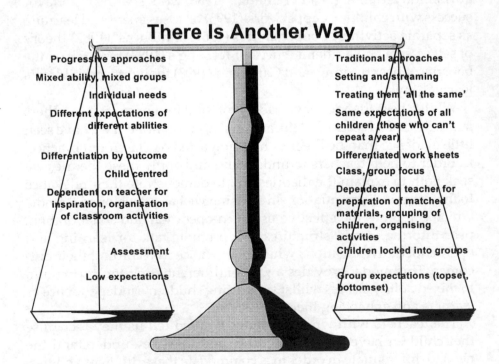

Figure 1.1   The scales diagram.

and teacher controlled traditionalists. We have come to describe this model as: 'There is Another Way': this way focuses on independent learning, skills training and on separating the learning activity from the assessment activity.

When considering the current polarised debate in education about whole class teaching or individual work, setting and streaming or mixed ability, and thinking about the way in which we usually teach, the authors envisaged a model to summarise their approach. They saw the debate and their own approach in the shape of a pair of scales with the arguments of the two polarised sides on either side and their way in the middle. This is outlined in Figure 1.1.

Progressive approaches (usually associated with child-centred learning.)	**Traditional approaches**
Mixed ability, mixed groups – this usually means that children are seated in mixed ability groups around tables.	Setting and streaming – grouping by ability.
Individual needs: children's individual needs are the focus, there is an expectation therefore that children will work at different rates, and produce work of different types and varying quality.	Children must be treated the same and equally, no allowances must be made, there are clear criteria and standards. In some European countries this means that children who fail simply repeat a year.
Children's prior experiences are the starting point for a lesson. This sometimes means that the curriculum is built around children's perceived needs, interests and environment. Topic work was an example of this.	The curriculum content is the starting point. The focus is on knowledge that has been prioritised and which all children need to experience.
Differentiation by outcome, where different standards of work are expected from children of different abilities.	Differentiation by task – teachers try to match the task to the ability of the child.
Differentiation by resource. Teachers set up activities in the room and try to 'extend' them by having conversations with the most able, and provide 'security' by explanations for the least able. This creates a need for more adults in the classroom.	Teachers have usually already sorted children into ability groups and may feel that there is no reason to differentiate further. Those who do prepare worksheets and different types of work for different abilities usually use text access techniques to help those with literacy difficulties. This is time consuming.

The two sides

Progressive approaches (usually associated with child-centred learning.)	**Traditional approaches**
Relaxed informal atmosphere where children are happy and encouraged to talk but talk will be on-task to teacher and off-task to peers. High achieving children will be interested but not stretched or challenged.	Tight formal structures, children not encouraged to talk. Strict routines, much whole class instruction and teaching. No talk for exploration or deeper understanding. Surface Learning the 'norm'. In these circumstances talk is likely to be off-task.
Low expectations usually result from the Differentiation by Outcome.	Low standards and 'refusal' or alienation can develop in children who are constantly given the 'easy' sheet or activity in Differentiation by Task.
Dependency and Learned Helplessness develop because the children are dependent on the teacher for inspiration, organisation of classroom activities and assessment feedback.	Learned Helplessness, negative self-belief and low self-esteem are the negative by-products for the children who are in the low ability group or who receive the low ability work. In our experience once children believe they are no good they cannot perform very well and are unable to do the work even if it is carefully matched to their ability level. Refusal to start 'the work' unless an adult helps them or nags them to write the date, draw a margin, write the question are examples of Learned Helplessness. (1978)

For both sets of teachers, those on the right and those on the left, variety and differences between children both in terms of ability and learning styles are seen as problems, usually to be resolved by 'extra resources.'

It is the authors' experience that children from both ends of the ability range can demonstrate enormous gains in learning if the material is presented in a different way. This happens when children see themselves as being equal in a classroom where difference is encouraged and valued rather than considered abnormal and a cause of extra work for everyone; and when self-belief is positive.

This other way sees variety and difference as an asset. It looks at children's differences and sees them as interesting forms of potential collaboration, with children providing complementary skills for one another. The resourcing issue is then a straightforward one of class size rather than resources for difference in ability.

Differentiation is about giving access and entitlement. It should also lead to an end to dependency. A variety of abilities should be seen as an asset and not a problem. The Model for Differentiation is a model based on collaboration between children with different styles and strengths and not on a hierarchy of abilities. Talk is the basis for differentiation, not tasks.

In our Model for Differentiation where talk and collaboration are the key, the teacher:

- structures learning and assessment so that children can learn through talk as well as reading and writing (Differentiation by Classroom Organisation).
- encourages the children to demonstrate their learning through any media they like, hence offering a variety of recording mechanisms (Differentiation by Outcome, Product).
- teaches children to help each other to set and reach targets and teach each other to improve their work through carefully structured peer tutoring (Differentiation by Paired Task).

This model sees an end to matching tasks to children and a beginning of children deciding for themselves what they need to achieve. This means that children are not repeating work that they can already do which is often an unfortunate consequence of focusing on the 'basics.'

It is through the separation of the learning and assessment that differentiation in this way becomes possible. This method frees up the recording during the learning and enables the child to record in any way they wish – any way that helps them to demonstrate what it is that they can do. It gets formal reading and writing, in the way that is required for assessment purposes, out of the way during the

The Model for Differentiation

Three Approaches to Differentiation

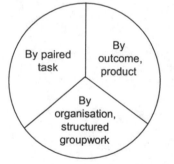

✦ By paired task:	Children work in supportive pairs to identify weaknesses, break down task into smaller steps and work on the steps
✦ By outcome: (product)	Usually workshops, varied stimuli, varied task, variety of recording every time
✦ By organisation: (structured	Groups working on same topic Equal and interchangeable recording systems

Figure 1.2   The model of differentiation.

learning process, and paradoxically this has the effect of increasing the amount of reading and writing that goes on in the lesson. This kind of reading and writing is incidental, purposeful and targeted. The amount of spontaneous learning increases enormously.

This model of differentiation rests on collaboration since each component: outcome, paired task, classroom organisation, either requires or encourages collaboration. The rationale for this collaboration for learning is presented in the next chapter.

Chapter 2

Collaboration:
a Model for Learning

In this chapter the following views are presented:
- collaboration leads to deep thinking;
- collaborative learning leads to independence of teacher and support teacher;
- deep thinking motivates all learners including children;
- the way that collaboration leads to deep thinking is through talk;
- the link between thought and language is detailed in the theories of Vygotsky;
- people feel supported in their learning through collaboration;
- low self-esteem can be challenged through collaboration and those with low self-esteem can come to value themselves and their achievements;
- the shared success that collaborating pairs experience helps to reduce the effects of negative attribution (those with low self-esteem attribute success to luck or chance or to their support teacher, and failure to themselves);
- matching of task and child's ability is inappropriate because it does not allow children to operate in their 'zone of proximal development';
- collaborative approaches to learning allow for a variety of structures and therefore help the teachers to pace their lessons.

Whilst writing this book the authors have talked to each other a great deal about differentiation and developed our thinking on the subject. We have also been talking about and reflecting on what happens when we work together, teach together and write together. This latter set of reflections has led to an examination of the process of our own thinking and learning. It is our belief that the talking to each other and the collaboration process has helped the deeper thinking we have arrived at in relation to differentiation. Without the collaboration this book would have been qualitatively different. The result of

Our own learning

this reflective thinking on both the learning process and differentiation is two models. The Model for Differentiation was outlined in the previous chapter, the Model for Learning which is based on collaboration is outlined below.

Writing books is not our job, it is our passion. We both have full time teaching jobs, we both have research commitments and we are both wives and mothers and so have many pulls on our time and attention. However, we write books because the teachers we teach ask us to, and because it is a way of reaching a large number of teachers to whom we cannot otherwise speak directly.

Writing books is hard. Each time at the outset we say 'It'll be easier this time', but it never is. In fact it seems to get harder. At first we believed this was because the issues we were dealing with were complex but we have come to realise that it is because the process of writing leads to deeper understanding. It seems that as we grapple with the issues that this deep thinking leads us to, then we enter an unravelling process where issues that had seemed straightforward become multi-faceted. Given that the writing is so hard we frequently question our reasons for doing it. It seems to be that we are driven to write in this way in order to develop our thinking through the collaborative process. Our evidence is the fact that we have written a book together about every two years.

The powerful motivation which we experience through our collaboration and which leads us to put ourselves and our families through a very painful process is most certainly not to be found in the end product as we rarely re-read our published material and indeed have both been in the situation of not even having a copy available to show to an enquiring teacher. The motivation must therefore be in the process of the collaborative writing, not in the product. The process includes:

- the acquisition of the insights that come through 'deep' thinking;
- the feeling of satisfaction when thoughts and ideas are clarified, sorted, ordered and we have a clear sense of 'learning.'

From our observations we think that this process is one that children go through too. The collaborative process becomes a motivator in itself as well as the activity.

Children's learning

Howard Gardner (1993) suggests that the reason why some children are underachieving is that the way they are being taught doesn't suit their learning style or their 'intelligence.' In addition Gardner suggests that most teaching that goes on in classrooms only results in a layperson's conceptual understanding or a rote or a routine understanding. He claims that it is rare for pupils to acquire a deep discipline understanding of a subject. His view is that children pick up the language of the discipline they are studying but they do not understand that they need to use that language to replace their lay conceptual framework. For example they may talk about 'force fields' and 'gravity' but when they kick a football they still think in terms of it being the foot that makes the ball move not the force. He recommends 'apprentice learning' as a way of helping children to increase their conceptual framework. We see this as being synonymous to pairwork and collaborative groupwork and therefore see collaboration as the best way of helping youngsters to genuinely absorb the new conceptual framework.

One way of accounting for the success of apprentice learning and collaborative learning in children is that when they explain their perceptions using the words from their own preferred intelligence, and then hear other people's points of view using words from a different type of intelligence, they may come to a new understanding and insight which can lead to them developing a deep 'discipline' conceptual framework.

The combination of theories like Gardner's and our own observations leads us to the conclusion that the real learning takes place when knowledge becomes understanding. The next step in learning is when understanding is transferred into a conceptual framework; this is deep learning. Factual knowledge and remembering information is surface learning. For us, surface learning is characterised by a number of activities that we ourselves have given children and which we often see teachers give to children; we call this busy work, work that keeps children occupied and quiet but does not challenge them. Colouring in, gap filling worksheets, some comprehension and cloze exercises are examples.

We are also putting forward the suggestion that when children experience the collaboration they are more likely to experience deep thinking which in itself is motivating and spurs them on. This means that the collaborative process has the potential to create the kind of independent 'ideal' learners that many teachers have described to us; children who ask questions, have a thirst or hunger for knowledge, children who want to find out more, know more, and do more.

Thus the activity that children do to learn is not as important as the *way* in which they are learning.

Collaboration is central to our Model for Learning, in other words people need to work with each other in order to learn most effectively. As a result of observing both the benefits of collaboration and the problems of isolation we have identified three key reasons for the success of collaboration in creating deeper thinking. The rationale for collaboration is that it helps learners to:
- develop their own thinking through talk;
- get support;
- value their achievements.

The way that collaboration leads to deep thinking

Developing thinking through talk

In addition to helping a wide range of pupils to express themselves, to demonstrate skills and understanding that others did not know they had, or expect them to have, and to work towards their true potential, the structures in differentiation by classroom organisation enable all children to work in their 'zone of proximal development.' (Vygotsky, 1962). For all of us this zone is our area of learning, the area where we move from the 'known to the unknown'. According to Vygotsky this can only be done through talk. What happens when the children come to problem solve through collaboration is that they realise in explaining something that in fact they have not thought out that part very clearly. This can often be seen in collaborative writing. When two children are placed together at one computer to write a report on the recent sports day, teachers will observe the fact that they continually stop typing in order to talk through and clarify what exactly they are going to write. They find that even though they thought they knew what they were going to write, the effect of sharing their perceptions of the event they are reporting results in an entirely new perspective for both children.

If the collaborative task set is not just a piece of factual recording but a reflective task requiring understanding as well as knowledge, for example the reasons for historical events occurring and their impact on life today, or the explanation of a scientific experiment, the new perspective that they gain often leads to a new understanding which can contribute to their developing conceptual framework. Therefore it is clear that through this talk children can develop both their own thinking and their conceptual framework. Being in a pair, children have to explain what they are thinking, what they think is the best idea and why.

Vygotsky's view was that language is vital for us to be able to think. What Vygotsky meant by the word 'think' was specific and different to when we say 'Well, I think . . .' For example: 'I think that Manchester United should have been given more time' is a viewpoint. 'I must remember to go to the supermarket for mum after school' is a remembering thought.

Vygotsky was talking about the thinking that we have when our understanding is unclear and hazy. For example, 'I know that water freezes and goes solid. I wonder if washing up liquid would freeze? I suppose it would if it were at freezing point, but aren't there different freezing points for things? Better ask Darren.' Vygotsky's zone of proximal development was to do with moving from the understanding we have when we are 'sure' to the understanding when we are 'not sure.' This is the area of the child's potential, the link between knowledge and understanding, and this zone is important. The knowledge that is sure and certain is knowledge which was already there. New learning whether it is factual or understanding is in the zone of proximal development. As this new learning becomes sorted and classified it becomes old learning and a new zone is reached. If the new knowledge is not sorted out there is no learning, the person stays with their old knowledge and frame, dimly aware of new words and facts but unable to make sense of them.

Vygotsky is clear that we can review and increase our own understanding of what we think, we can move from the 'unsure' to the sure through talk and through being helped by someone else's structured talk to reflect. What is also clear to the authors from their conversations with both adult students (teachers on accredited courses for instance) and child students is that it is very difficult to commit to paper thoughts which are not 'sure' or clear.

This explanation may account for the fact that some children never seem to progress through the spiral curriculum. Thus when they 'do' the water cycle two or three times in their years at school, instead of getting a deeper understanding they stay with the same understanding. When they are asked to take notes and write things down the notes do not add to their previous knowledge, the note taking is a task which gets done but does not contribute to the child's understanding. Thus if the child is allowed to talk they are more likely to come to a new and deeper understanding than if they take notes, even if the notes made at the time of the deeper understanding are not particularly full. The next time the child approaches this topic, if they have 'learnt' it properly they will progress.

Talk in this case then is a means to understand and develop our own thinking. This often happens when children are asked to work in pairs and to explain what it is they have understood after an experiment or a video or talk input. Vygotsky suggests that through the explaining both partners in the pairing come to realise what it is that they are thinking, clarify their thinking and understanding and sometimes come to new thoughts or concepts.

If children are not encouraged to talk or worse still told to 'stop talking and get on with their work' they may never come to understand their own thinking. 'We simply do not know how many people are frustrated in their learning by inability ever to express themselves adequately; or how many never develop intellectually because they lack the words with which to think and reason.' (Bruner, 1986)

Support

The support that children get when they work together is twofold. Firstly they get help in their thought and language development, secondly they get emotional support which helps their sense of self-worth and self-belief.

There is also support available for the pair in the following ways:
- the amount of work for any one person is reduced;
- provision of encouragement when difficulties arise;
- motivation through shared goals;
- motivation in not wanting to let the other person down.

An important aspect of this support is the relative safety of a pair. Compared to the whole group of thirty a pair is a secure place to try out ideas and risk expressing a new thought without fear of ridicule.

The suggestion by these authors is that learning, that is learning which is to do with understanding and forming concepts as opposed to the simple acquisition of knowledge, is risky and tentative and happens most productively when adults and peers are supporting the learner through this process. As Barnes says: 'Equal status and mutual trust encourage thinking aloud: one can risk inexplicitness, confusion and dead ends because one trusts in the tolerance of others. The others are seen as collaborators in a joint enterprise, rather than competitors for the teacher's approval.' (Barnes, 1977).

Bruner points out the importance of a type of talk which takes place between adults (typically though not exclusively mothers) and children. This he calls 'scaffolding'. It is the kind of language that supports the child but also allows them to make progress. Scaffolding has a supportive structure but retains open-endedness to encourage the learner to work independently when they are ready. He says scaffolding is 'a system of collaboration that represents the kind and quality of cognitive support which an adult can provide for a child's learning.' (Bruner, 1983).

However, he also says that both adults and children can provide this kind of support.

> If the child is able to advance under the tutelage of an adult, or a more competent peer, then the tutor or aiding peer serves the learner as a vicarious form of consciousness until such time as the learner is able to master his own actions through his own consciousness and control. (Bruner, 1985, p. 24)

An example of this scaffolding is a combination of paraphrasing and checking out together with probing and questioning.

> 'So the water goes in that hole and comes out as a river does it?'
> 'Well not as big as a river, more a trickly thing really.'
> 'A trickly thing?'
> 'Yeah, a sort of stream thing.'

This kind of supportive language enables the learner to develop their thinking, to move on, to come to a different kind of understanding

This scaffolding is not person specific; either in the pair may be scaffolding for the other, and they frequently swap roles, so that one is exploring and building on the other's scaffold then the next moment is scaffolding for their partner. In this respect it is a kind of 'piggy back' sharing of ideas with each partner taking it in turns to 'piggy back' for the other.

Another way in which the scaffolding can work, however, is in peer tutoring, where one partner explains things to the other, encouraging the learner to work things out for themselves along the way.

Scaffolding can also help to clarify one's ideas and improve one's understanding through talking with others who have a clearer picture. Blagg says that collaboration can help learners to reach their potential . He describes 'potential' in the quotation below where he links the Vygotsky 'zone of proximal development' with the 'scaffolding' of Bruner:

> The distance between the actual (mental) development level as determined by independent problem solving and the level of potential (mental) development as determined through problem solving under adult guidance or in collaboration with more capable peers. (Blagg, 1991, p. 4).

Additionally the collaboration can provide the child with confidence to try out learning in an independent way at a later time. 'What the child can do in a pair today they can do alone tomorrow.' (Bruner, 1985)

The other aspect of support is that of emotional support associated with self-esteem. Self-esteem is a term that is often used by teachers, but in our experience it is not always understood. The evidence of such a misunderstanding includes teachers complaining that some of their students have 'too high a self-esteem' or voicing an anxiety that if they as teachers try to improve the children's low self-esteem the children may stop trying, stop striving to get better results. For this reason we feel it is important to examine carefully the concepts covered by the word self-esteem.

Our own understanding of self-concept, self-esteem, academic self-concept and academic self-esteem has been shaped by our readings of the 'self' theorists: Coopersmith, 1967, and Rogers, 1961, and by the self education researchers: Purkey, 1970, Coopersmith, 1967, Burns, 1982, Lawrence, 1988, Gurney, 1988, Skaalvik, 1990; and by our own research and work with teachers, and by listening to children.

Our reading and experience has led us to the following understanding. Self-concept is shaped by the feedback from significant others. We come to an understanding of how good we are at something in relation to academic work, friendships, physique, and family because of the verbal and non-verbal cues that significant others around us give us. For example a boy who is very fair-haired and fair-skinned and rather chubby as a Year Five child may be called 'pouf' 'gay' and 'fatty' and feel he is unattractive physically to both boys and girls. He may in the end come to see himself as worthless overall because 'people don't like me.'

We also carry inside ourselves a view of how we ought to be – our ideal selves – a sense of 'if we were really good at . . . we would.' For example, a girl who is one of the best two swimmers in the school may feel she is 'no good at swimming' because at an evening swimming club she is not picked for the galas.

The discrepancy between the self-image and ideal self is our sense of self-worth, which is a measure of the amount we value ourselves in a given area. This sense of self-worth then acts as a filter on all our experiences. It becomes a self fulfilling prophesy and affects motivation. If I believe I am 'no good at swimming' I may stop trying so hard in the time trials and therefore find that my times are not as good as the others of my age and that I am not put in for a race. This confirms my sense that I am no good, even though the outside evidence is that only the best swimmers go to swimming club anyway.

Low self-esteem can be found both in 'bright children' and in children with 'learning difficulties.' We cannot know how children value themselves on the inside, therefore children who appear to have a great deal going for them: get good test results, have friends, collect awards for hobbies, have interested and supportive parents and siblings, may in fact be comparing aspects of themselves to an unrealistically high model, and may have consequential low self-esteem. What is apparent is that teachers alone cannot raise self-esteem. The authors have accepted Coopersmith's (1967) findings that the three shapers of academic self-esteem are parents, peers and teachers in equal parts and have worked with teachers to ensure that both teachers and peers give those with low self-esteem positive feedback. In these circumstances the self-esteem of children does increase. The only way we have achieved this targeted feedback for children with low self-esteem from their peers is to train and reward all the children for giving each other positive feedback. This is a long, slow process in some school environments but it pays off in the long term.

In summary then the authors have found that it is vital that peers in the classroom are consistently supportive to each other both verbally and non-verbally to improve self-esteem. Collaboration provides the right kind of feedback to enhance self-esteem in this way:

- positive feedback is given throughout the collaboration by the other person;
- the possibility of failure in completing the task is reduced;
- positive feedback from both the teacher and other peers through success in the task is experienced by both partners;
- positive self-esteem is not only important for academic achievement and the emotional well being of the individual child, it also affects the general discipline and cultural norms in the classroom. Children with low self-esteem are likely to behave badly. They do not like or value themselves therefore they are not likely to value others.

Through the collaborative structures the children with low self-esteem will start to be valued by the other children, then to value themselves and cease to engage in negative behaviours such as ridiculing anyone who appears more different, less worthy or an easier target for bullying than themselves. Our evidence is that there will be an actual decrease in negative behaviours as well as a marked increase in positive behaviours.

In this way collaborative pairwork helps to improve classroom climate. The elimination of the ridiculing, put downs, giving negative feedback and other negative behaviour from those children who have low self-esteem to anyone who seems to be different means that the victims no longer get victimised. These victims include those who are different because of their race, their gender, their academic success, high motivation or physical difference.

Valuing achievements

When children collaborate together there is a greater chance that both will value the task and the product of the task. They are less likely to 'rubbish' the task because by doing so they will 'rubbish' their partner also. Thus work on valuing each other is an essential prerequisite to valuing the task. Children with low self-esteem are likely to be the ones with negative attributions, that is, they are likely to attribute a successful task to others or luck and a poor quality task to themselves. Teachers can explicitly teach children to attribute success to themselves in the way of Marie Louise Craske, 1988, a researcher-teacher who retrained children to attribute their success in maths to their own level of effort rather than to the teacher or chance. Through collaboration children can be helped to ascribe specific roles and therefore feel a clear sense of responsibility when they are successful in their task.

Type of task

The task given makes very little difference to the nature of the support offered by pairwork. However the way in which the task is presented for the pairwork will effect the success of the task itself. Practically any task that would normally be offered as an individual piece of work can be given as a paired activity. There are however a few minor changes that need to be made to the structuring of the activity in order to ensure successful collaboration on the task. For paired activities there are two underlying principles which need to be taken into account. These are:
- a joint product;
- collaboration as a criterion for success.

Joint product

The task should require a joint product. Instead of two children working together and both producing individual worksheets, for example, they should be given one worksheet between them and asked to complete it together. In that way the task itself actively encourages the work to be shared, for instance, children taking it in turns to write answers to questions. This turn taking should be made explicit by the teacher asking the children to work in this way. It is to

Structuring the collaboration

be remembered that we are dealing with the learning process here and not the assessment of children's learning. Therefore the fact that there is only one product between two is not important because the focus at this point in the learning process is not the ability of the individual child to produce work on their own for assessment purposes.

Collaboration as a criterion for success

Criteria for success include helping each other. If this is made clear to the children and they are taught the skills outlined below, then it is possible for the teacher to deem a piece of work incomplete if the task has been done but there is no evidence that they have both contributed. In fact this addresses the concern of teachers when pairwork is suggested. Their previous experience of pairwork is that in many cases one child does all the work and the other sits by or even wanders off. This is either because one is so dominant that they do not let the other one in because of fear that the other will spoil it or because one perceives himself to be no good. Making collaboration part of the task overcomes this difficulty and helps the conversation between the pair to focus on the discussion about why the collaboration is difficult and how they can work together. The best way for teachers to make their concerns about this aspect clear to the children is to refuse to accept and mark work that has no evidence of collaboration. Such evidence can be gathered either through using the threes structure where one child acts as an observer and gives feedback on the collaboration; or by there being evidence in terms of two sets of handwriting, or by the teacher walking round and observing and possibly putting a mark or comment on their pairs work to the effect that she has witnessed collaboration. Or 'spotters' may be used to do the same thing. Spotters are child observers who go round the whole class observing rather than being attached to just one pair. (See Figures 2.1 and 2.2.)

Our experience has demonstrated that when a co-operative climate prevails and collaboration is rewarded by teacher praise then children very naturally begin to help each other. In order for their collaborative skills to increase beyond those naturally encouraged by the joint task and the teacher's recognition of collaboration as worthy and important the children will need some specific training in the skills of helping each other more effectively. Figure 2.3 shows a self assessment sheet which can be used during this skills training.

Our experience of collaboration is that children need to:
- come to know each other;
- then learn to help one another;
- begin to reward and give positive feedback to each other;
- finally they are able to collaborate in an equal partnership and experience the academic success that support in a pair can bring.

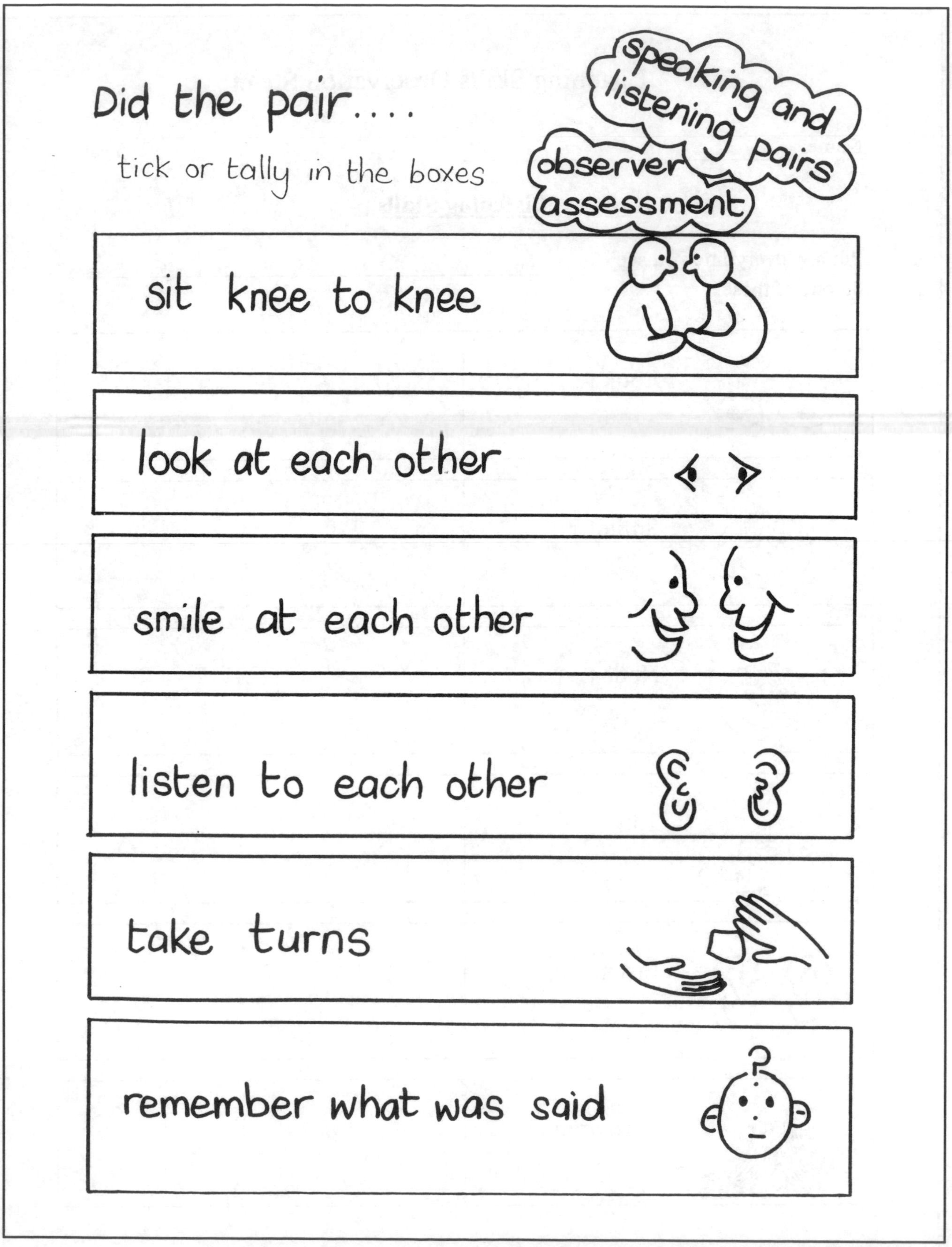

Figure 2.1 Observer's assessment sheet (© Helen Newton).

Listening Skills Observation Sheet

Name: _____   Year 1

Listening Skills

Put a ✓ everytime you see
do one of these......   _____

👀 Look	
😊 Smile	
↕😊↕ Nod	
😮 Talk (Hello)	
👂👂 Listen	
Turn around	

Figure 2.2   Observer's sheet for listening skills.

18

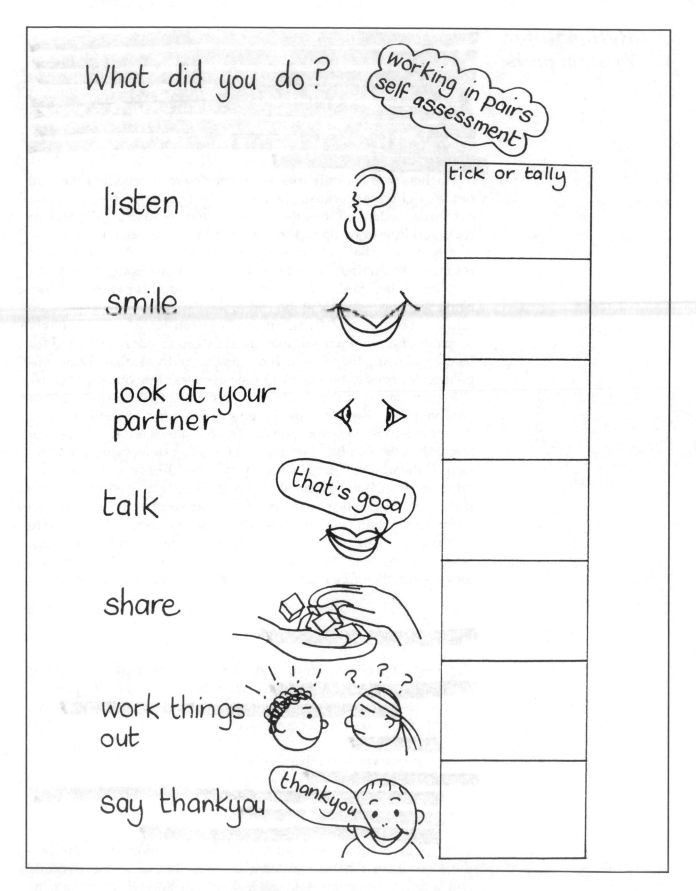

Figure 2.3 Self assessment sheets (© Helen Newton).

Rationale for random pairs

Our belief in pairwork and collaboration leads us to the conclusion that random pairing is an essential pre-requisite for any of the work in this book to take place. For us it is the first skill in the skills training programme. We are aware of teachers' own misgivings about this but we have come to believe that there can be no learning for significant numbers of children in the class if teachers allow friendship pairs to dominate classroom organisation and do not actively intervene in the social relationships of children.

Teachers who use only friendship pairs have noticed that they are not very effective because one side of the friendship pair becomes overly dependent on the other. This is often because the dependent child gets little or no opportunity to be a teacher or leader but is constantly stuck in the role of receiver of help. A common solution to this is to split the children up and not allow them to work together whilst they are in that class. This sometimes results in this pair of children being separated entirely at the end of the year when new classes are formed. The loss of a friend in this way can have an exceedingly negative effect on their self-esteem. They can also feel punished for helping or being helped which means that individualism and competition is prized at the expense of the deep learning outlined below.

Rather than split the children our recommendation is the use of random pairs. This is because it helps children to come to know and therefore be able to work with everyone in the class. If they do not know the others in the class all they have is a stereotypical impression of them, which makes it easy for them to fear one another's differences, including academic success. The fear itself often gives rise to ridicule and negative comments which contribute to creating a fairly hostile climate in the classroom. In such a climate it is unlikely that children will take risks with their learning, therefore children underachieve. It is also unlikely that the children will voice their weaknesses, therefore little practice and improvement takes place.

Organisation into random pairs

Organising the children into random pairs can be done very simply. Cards are usually best initially, either published cards with pictures of animals so the child finds someone with a matching picture, or teacher produced cards. These may be:
- coloured cards;
- card with coloured shapes stuck on;

or, if the children can read:
- names of famous couples e.g. Romeo and Juliet, Meg and Mog;
- pairs of objects: cup and saucer;
- homonyms, e.g. pair and pare, their and there.

Later, as the children get used to this way of working they can produce sets of cards that are related to the topic they are doing; pyramid and Giza, centurion and soldier. Or simply two drawings that are the same or are cut in half.

Our research has shown that contrary to teachers' expectations younger age children find learning to collaborate easier than older age children who seem to need to unlearn some competitive habits brought about by allowing children to work only as individuals or in friendship pairs. To overcome this difficulty with older children our recommendation is that random pairs is introduced little and often and that children continue to work in friendship pairs for the times in between random pairs. The friendship pair is an ideal place to begin to teach the children to use the skills such as helping, encouraging and explaining which they need in order to become collaborative workers. Such work changes the nature of the friendship pair towards a collaborative partnership rather than one where one person becomes increasingly dependent on the other.

Teachers must also be prepared for this way of working to produce a more noisy environment, as children are required to talk to each other. The feelings that this can engender might be quite uncomfortable for the teacher initially. If teachers are concerned about the type of talk they should go around and listen or ask the children what they are talking about. Teachers who work in this way report that they find that the talk is entirely on task and that the noise is 'busy noise' not disruptive noise. Teachers must beware that they do not stop using the structures because they feel at first that they are not working. The skills develop through taking part in the structures as well as through the specific skills teaching.

Summary

Collaborative learning leads to independence. What we have outlined in this chapter is our understanding of how children think and learn. This has implications for teachers who need to consider how to include children in the planning of the lesson and how to help children to be involved in working things out for themselves. They also need to recognise the prior learning of children. We want teachers to understand children's construction of knowledge and not assume that children do not know anything because they cannot do the tasks which we set them.

Chapter 3

Planning and Assessment

What has been outlined so far in this book are the authors' beliefs which can be summarised as follows:

- Children working collaboratively is vital because it stops them being dependent on the teacher or other adults and therefore helps them to become independent learners.
- Skills training to work in pairs, as a group, or as an independent learner, need to be specifically planned and taught.
- Time should be allowed for refining learning and practising skills.
- Matching tasks and children's abilities as a way of differentiating is inappropriate because it does not move children through their 'zone of proximal development' for their learning. Practising the 'basics' needs to happen at another time, not during the learning.
- Expecting different outcomes from children of different abilities as a way of differentiating is also inappropriate as it leads to low expectations.
- The way children feel about themselves in relation to the others in the classroom affects their motivation, which in turn influences the quality of their work. Using the collaboration structures enables children to come to know others, to value others and so to value themselves and their work.

Below we summarise our beliefs about planning assessment:

- Learning and assessment are two different things.
- Teachers should plan their lessons in ways that focus on the learning objective.
- The tasks then emerge from the planning (the task should not be the starting place).
- Assessment tasks should be identified and take place after the children have had an opportunity to reach the learning objective.

The reason that teachers may well feel daunted by this view is because they:

- feel anxious about 'getting through' the National Curriculum content. Many teachers feel it is unfair to expect 'their' children to do the National Curriculum when these children have such difficulties with reading and writing.
- believe that the OFSTED inspection process is unfair because 'their' children are not starting on a level playing field because of the home backgrounds. Despite this sense of injustice teachers also fear that the inspectors will 'tell them off' because they are not 'doing things properly.' This often leads to teachers being preoccupied with providing paper evidence for the inspection and teaching 'safe' lessons which paradoxically do not stretch the children.
- feel the League Table comparison of results is not fair because 'their' children did not start from the same place as other children but they do not want to let their children down so they focus on teaching children the basics.
- are understandably focused on what they are going to teach them rather than what the pupils are going to learn.

As a result they focus on designing the task and when children cannot do the task they assume this is because the children lack knowledge as well as skills.

We are aware of the fact that the changes we are asking teachers to make are difficult in the light of the very real fears, anxieties and low self-esteem that many teachers experience. However we are convinced that because of the interest that most teachers have in helping their children do well teachers will read this chapter and 'have a go.'

Assessment – a change in teacher attitude

There is a difference between setting a task for learning and setting a task for assessment. Many teachers confuse the two. It is possible that this confusion has not been helped by the introduction of teacher assessment alongside SAT assessment. Teacher assessment is seen as an ongoing process throughout the year culminating in an end of term or year statement of the child's achievement. This has led to some teachers feeling that all activities in the classroom are potentially assessment opportunities. Teachers have told us that teacher assessment is the reason they reject pairwork and collaboration. They cannot see how they can let children work together and carry out individual assessment at the same time

The authors recognise this difficulty and that is why they find it more useful to see the ongoing classroom activities as learning opportunities, with specific assessment activities that are designed to assess children's achievements against the learning objectives used periodically throughout the year. It is only these assessment activities that need to be carried out by an individual child working alone, or with the amount of support given and noted by the teacher. All other learning activities can be performed in pairs or groups. The authors also find that if teachers make:

- the learning objectives;

- the criteria for success with the learning activities;
- the assessment activities;
- the criteria for success for the assessment activities

clear to the children, then the children get better marks in their assessment.

This is fairly obvious but is being stated regularly because in our experience these components are not made clear to the children. They are usually in a teacher's head or on their scheme of work, they may be mentioned in passing but they are not being spelt out to children in such way that children can tell us when we ask them. These components need to be written on the whiteboard in language that children can understand and discussed by the children regularly.

Planning – changing teacher focus

The change in focus we are asking teachers to make is a move away from the task towards:

- the learning objective for each lesson;
- a variety of approaches to recording;
- skills for children's independence.

We recognise that our model of differentiation means planning and teaching in a different way. This change may seem daunting at a time when teachers are stressed by the curriculum, the amount of recent change, the pressure of OFSTED inspection and league tables and public criticism. Additionally teachers may feel overwhelmed by the number of different skills that children will need to work in this way. It may seem easier to stay as they are. However, these skills were always needed by children but were often not addressed until the children were struggling towards independence as learners in the secondary setting. For example when children lack the skills to either carry out the task in the way the teacher intended or to articulate their problems with the task and get some help from peers who could help them they tend to engage in 'avoidance behaviours.' The authors have observed these behaviours in many classrooms. Individual children might either refuse to do a task, or avoid it by not having the right equipment, or destroy the task by using their eraser so vigorously they rip their work in two pieces. In this situation the teacher would understandably find themselves in conflict with the children. This conflict is always stressful.

The effect of using the strategies outlined in this book and planning to increase their use to all subject areas will result in a change in the type of preparation that the teacher does on a day to day basis. This change is from preparing the task in detail, e.g. preparing the worksheets, gathering up equipment, to detailed long term and day-to-day planning and the constant review of creative alternatives to recording. When the teacher prepared the task in detail they were often involved in conflicts with the children, arising from the time and emotional investment they had put into designing what they felt was the best task to meet that child's assessed needs. What seems to happen when this change in focus takes place is that the teacher no longer has an emotional investment in the task prepared and therefore can help the children to find their own way to do the task.

There is a difference between organising the task, which is 'how' the children are going to achieve learning and telling them 'what' they need to learn, which is the learning objective. In being less prescriptive and more flexible about the task, the 'how,' and very specific about the learning objective, the 'what,' teachers free children to work in their preferred learning style whilst ensuring that they are able to achieve on the given curriculum.

Time is the reason so many teachers feel that they cannot differentiate whether it is by task or outcome or in the collaborative way that the authors are recommending. This is because teachers see differentiation as extra and not part of the delivery of the curriculum. The change in focus away from planning the task to planning the learning objective, assessment activity and skills training for working together actually creates time because of the simple act of deciding what it is we want children to learn in terms of: knowledge, facts, understanding, particular skills and conceptual frame, which leads to a prioritisation of learning.

We have found that teachers who work in this way report a massive increase in the time available to:

- talk with children;
- assess the children's progress;
- teach whole classes and
- help children to acquire new information.

They also find that there is an increase in their own enjoyment of teaching. What they say is 'I am teaching for the first time'. What they report is that they are no longer spending their time sorting out the endless minor disputes between children, dealing with avoidance of the task or sorting out the organisational details of each and every task as the children take on more and more responsibility for these things. We call this the 80-20 rule. That is, when children are doing eighty per cent of the work and the teacher is doing twenty per cent of the work you have achieved the correct balance. Children have eighty per cent of the time involved in learning and so are 'on task' far more often and consequently learn more, more quickly. Many teachers are working very hard and doing eighty per cent in preparation, organisation and supervision and are very tired as a result. The children meanwhile can only ever do twenty per cent because that is all that is left. They are bound to underachieve, get bored and act disruptively.

The new approach to planning means focusing on giving children choice. Some teachers are doubtful about their children's ability to make a choice. The authors have found that all children, including those with severe learning difficulties are capable of making a choice if we give it to them. However some children are unskilled because of

Time

Getting started

25

lack of practice. This is often a good place to start; simply by offering alternatives which address a wider range of learning styles. The teachers we have taught have found it helpful to ask themselves the question: 'This is how we normally structure it but how else could the children do this activity?'

Changing our teaching practice and our way of thinking is difficult and teachers need to give themselves plenty of time to gain experience in thinking about differentiation in this way. We recommend that teachers try out some of the illustrated ideas and then begin to plan one lesson per day at first in this way. This allows teachers to gain in confidence. We have found that as the teacher becomes familiar with planning and teaching through differentiation by outcome for one subject then they begin to feel confident to plan other subject areas using the same principles. Many teachers find it helpful to begin with either their own area of expertise or the curriculum area which they feel most lends itself to this way of working.

We suggest that teachers begin by planning the differentiation of one topic at first. We have found that because both teachers and children need some security it is best to retain other, more familiar ways of working and gradually add in more and more differentiation by organisation, outcome and paired task. Whilst it is a good idea to recall activities within this topic that have been successful in the past, when planning a topic with this model the difference is the adaptation of activities so that there is a focus on learning and collaboration.

The next step in the planning is to deal with resources. Again in order to ensure that there is enough time for skills training this resource planning needs to be done in advance. It is also helpful if resource gathering is done by a team of teachers so that the load is spread. Once the resources are gathered it is important to plan when each class will be using the material so that for example only 30 children need access to the history resources on a Thursday afternoon and not 120. Team planning combined with flexibility, for example being prepared to change Maths on Mondays afternoons so that all the children can be taught Tudor dancing by the 'guest visitor', can greatly multiply the effectiveness of any one resource. In fact team planning does more than 'spread the load.'

Team teaching

Planning with other teachers has many advantages. In the same way that talking helps children to clarify their ideas, the process of talking in a team helps teachers to clarify issues associated with the topic. These issues are not just organisational problems but conceptual ones too. It is clear to us that most teachers have hazy concepts in some areas of the curriculum. In order to be clear about assessment and learning objectives teachers need to clear this haze in the interests of conceptual understanding. The idea of 'learning along with the children' or keeping two pages ahead of them is acceptable in terms of detailed knowledge but not in relation to concepts. Discussions in team planning therefore need to explicitly discuss the concepts that teachers expect the children to acquire and ensure that everyone in the team has a similar and shared conceptual base. In this way there is a clear staff development aspect to the team planning. Managers can ensure that this additional aspect of team planning is taking place by sitting in on team meetings or asking for outline programmes of team planning meetings and requiring a discussion on the conceptual understanding aspect. The three questions that teachers need to constantly ask each other and themselves when planning are:

- What is it the children need to learn? (knowledge, skills, understanding, learning objective)
- How will we know that they have learned it? (assessment activity)
- This is how we normally do it, but how else could the children do it to reach the same end point?

Once teachers start to share and to challenge one another in the planning stage and experience the 'new idea' that collaborative work can bring, they are more likely to want to team teach and to use their fellow teacher as a confidante or mentor at the end of the lesson. In this way they get help in dealing with the mixed bag of feelings that we all have at the end of a teaching session, especially if a youngster has been particularly challenging. This is how teacher stress can be effectively managed through team teaching.

Planning a stepped approach

The authors have come to see the planning for differentiation as comprising a series of steps in planning. When we examine our own planning we find that we need to go through the following:

1. Select a topic or subject.
2. Prioritise the learning for that topic in conjunction with other teachers.
3. Select the aspects to be assessed from the prioritised learning and devise assessment and recording activities.
4. Decide on the learning objectives for each lesson or group of two or three lessons and in parallel decide on a skills training programme, starting with pairwork and listening skills.
5. Either plan a new activity or adapt a known activity which:
   - uses one type of differentiation covered in this book;
   - meets the learning objective;
   - is suitable for the present skills level of the children.
6. Plan the lesson for pace and variety using the 'Three Part Lesson' format.
7. Plan for breadth and balance.
8. Record and keep evidence.

1. Select a topic or subject

Teachers need to start by selecting a topic they have been successful with in the past. A topic might be a strand of the National Curriculum subject e.g. Electricity from Science. Or it may be a cross curricular theme such as Mini Beasts. The selection will depend upon the whole school plan for any particular age group. It is important that there is collaboration between members of the same year group team and liaison with the teacher of the years above and below. In this way the teacher can prioritise the key learning to be addressed in the knowledge that other areas not prioritised this year will be addressed in subsequent years. This removes the pressure to try to teach every aspect of the topic in one year. For example, if the subject is history and the topic for that year is the Tudors, teachers may decide that 'chronology and range and depth of historical knowledge and understanding' will be taught by every teacher, in every year group. They may then decide that whilst one year group prioritises the key historical skill of 'historical enquiry' another year group in the key stage will prioritise 'organisation and communication of historical information' and a third year group will focus on 'interpretation'. They may well leave the 'use of primary source material' and 'the discussion of bias' to Year Six. In this way the key elements will be covered over the key stage, just as the study units are.

2. Prioritise the key learning for a topic, with other teachers

As stated above, the important part of planning for differentiation is prioritising. Eventually this has to be done for every subject that is to be taught during the year. However the starting point is the prioritised strand from step one.

When teaching a strand of the curriculum many teachers find that they run out of time and this often results in the children feeling fed up and rushed and the teacher feeling frustrated. To plan effectively so that the teacher does not run out of time she needs to be absolutely clear about what it is she wants the children to know, and do, by the end of a topic and the time frame for this. As stated, this process begins with a prioritisation of skills, knowledge, understanding and concepts. Such prioritisation, whilst undoubtedly challenging for teachers, means that the level of detail, or the amount of practice for a skill, that the children can have on that topic can be determined. This makes it far more likely that the activities will:

- cover the curriculum content;
- give the children time to complete tasks;
- give the children time to develop the skills to improve in these tasks in the given time.

This enables teachers to plan the assessment at the beginning of the topic. We have found in our own teaching that stating these three components in 'child-speak' helps us to be specific which helps everyone else involved: parents, children, managers, classroom assistants and adult helpers, and other teachers, to understand what is required. The principles of behaviourism are helpful here. Behaviourism rests on the principle of being specific: being specific means identifying a behaviour that is observable and possibly quantifiable. For example a teacher may say to the children:

> By the end of this lesson I want you to be able to name the bones in the body. There are ten that you need to know the proper scientific term for. By the end of next lesson I want you to know where they are in the body. By the end of the third lesson I want you to be able to explain how the bones move to make us walk. Your assessment task will be to label a picture of the body with the names of ten bones and to explain the walking process. You will also need to know how to paraphrase. This will be assessed by a peer watching you with an observation schedule.

The way in which a teacher selects a differentiation strategy to help the children with these learning objectives and assessment tasks will then depend on the balance of activities for the day and the skill level of the children.

3. Select the aspects to be assessed from the prioritised learning, devise assessment and recording activities

As stated, there is a difference between assessment tasks and reviewing learning objectives. The learning objectives are small targets, building towards the whole skills and concepts package for that topic. These learning objectives should be checked through reviewing activities planned into each lesson or series of lessons. The assessment task should address the key learning which we have defined as the prioritised skills, knowledge, understanding and concepts for this topic. This means that an assessment task takes place at the end of a piece of learning not as part of the teaching and learning process.

In planning relevant assessment teachers should ask themselves the following questions:

- what do I want them to know?
- what do I want them to be able to do?
- what do I want them to be able to write in a test?

The authors have found that they can plan for assessment activities easily but find identifying learning objectives difficult and other teachers have endorsed this experience. This tells us that we have been assessing children too much without allowing them the space to learn. This preoccupation with assessment is likely to be because we see assessment results as a measure of our own effectiveness as teachers. The paradox is that *as we move away from this preoccupation and create the space for children to learn*, so their assessment results go up and we are seen as 'good' teachers.

These assessments can take the form of open or closed tasks. For example:

- *open ended tasks* which the children know about in the beginning so that they can collect and select work ready to demonstrate what they know and can do. Example:

To produce a written or audio taped guide to a real or imaginary Tudor house which reflects the way the building and the artefacts in the house show what it was like to live in Tudor times and how the main events in that period relate to this.

- *closed tasks* which address the key historical facts about an event or period. This can be done as a traditional question and answer test but there are alternatives. For example:

Statements about the family tree of the Tudors which can be separated into true and false facts by the children or a list of arguments referring to the need for the reformation of the church which children can sort into for and against as for a debate.

This latter example reduces the problem of written tasks not always being appropriate for all children and the difficulty therefore of assessing historical understanding through a written test.

Therefore it is clear that teachers do not need an assessment task that assesses every single small step in the learning process. Teachers do not have to 'do assessment tasks' or even make the children 'record' in written sentences; instead lessons can be concluded with the children's own learning review. Learning review is discussed in Chapters 5 and 6, 'Differentiation by Paired Task' and 'Differentiation by Classroom Organisation'.

Once the learning objectives and assessment activities have been identified and written into the planning, then these should be shared with the children. In addition, children need to be told what 'a good answer' is like. For many children this question is never addressed. They know they are 'no good at it' but they do not know why and so do not know how to improve. This means that teachers need to think about the way they mark and assess work and share this with children in advance of the assessment activity so that the children can plan to improve their work. Again team work helps here as the team can act as a moderating body when discussing the criteria for success. The criteria need to be explicit and specific. For example the teacher may say to the children: 'to get high marks you need to use the names of all the Greek gods and all the other characters in the story. The more names you use the higher marks you will get.' The children then know that it is important to learn the Greek names for their myth and legend story.

4. Decide on the learning objectives for each lesson or group of two or three lessons and in parallel decide on a skills training programme, starting with pairwork and listening skills

This planning of learning objectives means that whilst the discussion may still focus on decisions regarding the content such as whether to include Greek Gods or way of life of Greek citizens, the focus changes. The selection for the content is based upon a different set of criteria. Instead of the teachers selecting on the basis of what they are going to cover in the content of the curriculum, they are making decisions about what is important for everybody to learn. The differentiation through talk is an acceptance that every child may not cover every aspect of the study of the Ancient Greeks but that all will be engaged in the key learning elements. This means there is equal access for all to the curriculum. For example if the study unit is Ancient Greeks and the key elements prioritised are:

1. historical knowledge and understanding;
2. historical enquiry;

then the learning objective will be for the children to 'demonstrate their knowledge of the Ancient Greek way of life using a range of sources of information.' The skills training programme could then be 'listening and clarifying, then reporting back the information heard.'

These skills are crucial when anyone is required to share information. Therefore even if children need basic pairwork skills at this time, such as turn taking, the teacher will need to pay attention to the skills training for information sharing as well because it is so necessary for the historical topic.

These learning objectives for content and skills will then form the basis of the planning for the task as outlined in point 5 below.

5. Either plan a new or adapt a known activity using one form of the differentiations covered in this book

The activity needs to meet the learning objective and be in line with the present skills level of the children.

After having decided which particular aspect of knowledge and understanding and historical enquiry is to be prioritised, an activity will need to be selected which allows children to acquire experience of this. For example the focus might be 'knowledge of the Greek Pantheon,' gained by 'using secondary source materials'. The skills focus may be to 'listen and clarify information.' The activity is then fairly straightforward. It is for the children to find out about Greek gods using books and telling each other what they have discovered. The next decision is about the way in which the activity will be carried out. Traditionally most teachers would structure this as an individual exercise and would 'scaffold' for children through the worksheet which would contain key questions and words to help and direct them. Differentiation through talk focuses on talking before writing.

The children need to be told before they start that their assessment activity will be to 'write about the Greek gods using their names'. In this instance the teacher might select a rainbow structure, where the children are organised into random groups of four, each group using reference books to find information on the one Greek god which their group has been allocated. In these groups they would work in pairs to listen and clarify what they are going to share in their rainbow groups. They would then regroup, by colour, and share their findings with the new group members. Again they will listen and clarify. In this way they will have gained knowledge of several gods in the Pantheon whilst using a secondary historical source to list the information, and practised listening and clarifying.

The children can then be asked to 'make notes' in any way that will help them to remember what they have learned. These note-taking methods can include cartoon and stick men annotated drawings as well as writing sentences. They are now well placed to prepare themselves for the assessment.

6. Plan the lesson for pace and variety using the Three Part Format

Teachers are used to planning variety throughout the day and throughout the week but if we acknowledge that children have different learning styles then it is important to plan for variety throughout the lesson, and to invite the children to use and openly discuss their different learning styles within the structure we provide.

A strategy that we have found useful when helping teachers to use our model of differentiation is to think of the lesson as being in three parts: *the opening* which is the focus session, *the middle* which is where the main activities will take place and *the end* which we think should be used for reviewing.

a. The opening
This is a focusing time at the beginning of the lesson. Traditionally this is a whole class question and answer session. It is an introduction of a new topic or a review of 'where we got to last time.' It is an orientation period, so that the children can remember what they were last doing on this and where they had got to.

Planning Grid

Begin: Focus:	Knowledge Concepts	Review Target Set
Pairs Sharing Circle Brainstorm Fours Self + Topic	Fish Bowl Workshops Peer Tutoring Video Interviews Drama	Pairs Learning Circle 3's 4's

Figure 3.1 Plan the lesson for pace and variety.

For this review or for the initial introduction we recommend pairwork despite the fact that this is usually done as whole class teaching. Pairs is a safe place and enables more children to really think, reflect and plan what they may be going to do this lesson or what they already know about this topic. This type of focusing pairwork helps the children to feel confident about their prior learning and therefore to build on that prior learning. It helps children to articulate their current conceptual understanding and therefore to be open to challenges to that understanding. For example, some Year Two children, when discussing electricity in an opening random pairs exercise, identified matches and batteries as being electrical items. Considering the fact that the authors know some adults who think that electricity 'leaks' out of plugs we felt that it was most useful to have enabled the children to voice these misconceptions so that they could be corrected. The authors' experience suggests that the traditional whole class methods fail to uncover such misconceptions.

b. The learning activity

The middle main part is the knowledge, skills, concepts and tasks section. At the beginning of this section there would be whole class teaching for instructions and learning objectives to be given. This might be followed by a demonstration of a particular skill. For example:

- observational drawings;
- where to put a comma;
- note taking;
- tally charts.

This would then be followed by an activity which helps the children to learn and practice these skills. For this a whole range of structures for differentiation may be used:

- pair-work;
- group-work;
- workshops.

These are outlined in detail in the chapters on differentiation by outcome (Chapter 4) and by classroom organisation (Chapter 6).

c. The learning review

The end of the lesson should be a period of review. OFSTED recognise that this is usually absent as their inspection reports have highlighted the importance of monitoring and evaluation. This is a new development in teaching; the authors have only recently introduced it into their own teaching, but they can vouch for its effectiveness.

The better and more organised teachers have a 'pack away time' at the ends of lessons and possibly a 'story time' at the end of the day. Few teachers have been taught how to organise the children to reflect on their own learning at the end of the lesson.

This reviewing is best undertaken by ensuring that there is a time at the end of each lesson, not just for clearing up the classroom mess but for children to organise their messy thoughts. This enables children to reorientate themselves from the end of a completed or nearly completed task and turn their faces towards the next step.

If the children are new to reviewing lessons then we have found that it is necessary to teach them. A simple way to do this is to begin with a learning circle at the end of a lesson where children in a whole class circle are asked to state one thing they have learned or can do now that they didn't or couldn't at the beginning of the lesson. They may need to prepare for this learning circle by rehearsing their answers in pairs first. When they get used to this strategy the pairwork can be lengthened into a more reflective turn taking exercise where the pairs take their partners through the following stem statements:

- what I enjoyed was . . .
- what I didn't enjoy as much was . . .
- what I have learned is . . .
- what I found easy was . . .
- what I found difficult was . . .
- the point at which I actually got stuck was . . .

Children can also practise asking open questions in these reviewing pairs. They can even be observed by a peer using an observation schedule and receive appropriate feedback so that they can refine their questioning skills.

To encourage more long-term reviewing skills teachers can write the lessons taught that week onto cards and place in a bag. Children can then pass the bag around and pick out a card denoting a particular lesson (playtimes and lunch-times as well as after-school activities can also be included). Each child is to say something about:

- what they did in that lesson
- what they achieved
- what they liked about it
- what they found difficult or
- what they found memorable.

Not only is this excellent training for reviewing and target setting but such a whole class circle creates a cohesiveness within the classroom which engenders peer support as other children recognise each others' difficulties. The teacher too gains greater insights into the difficulties which children may be having which may have otherwise been undetected.

The staged process above allows the children to move towards the point where they can work in pairs to answer the following more complex reflective questions:

- What strategies have you used this lesson?
- What have you learned?
- Have you achieved the learning objectives?
- What target are you going to set for yourself?
- What is your plan for the next lesson?

The teacher's planning stages are summarised in Figure 3.2.

In the authors' experience spending time on this reviewing process makes the 'focusing' at the beginning of the following lesson shorter and more effective.

Planning the Topic

1. Select area for assessment from programmes of study in liaison with other staff

2. Plan these areas over a year

3. Plan each term in detail

4. Plan each activity to have **variety**

5. Write learning objectives and assessment tasks in 'child-speak,' share with the children

Figure 3.2 Summary of planning stages.

Once this reviewing time is clearly established it is relatively straightforward to introduce the ideas outlined in 'Differentiation by Paired Task', (Chapter 5).

7. Plan for breadth and balance throughout the week

Plans for a day do not need to ensure that there is a balance of subject areas covered providing there is a balance throughout the week. This allows the teacher to plan whole days where children can pursue a project without being interrupted by changes in subject. This is really important when art work, technology or drama are being addressed as these subjects often benefit enormously from chunks of time being devoted to them so that children can develop their ideas fully, then revise their ideas before they do a final presentation.

What a teacher might wish to ensure is that there is a balance between types of activity to ensure that a day is not dominated for instance by writing, even if the writing is for four different subject areas, but that oracy, drawing, thinking, physical making, planning etc. are in evidence in every subject with writing tasks short, focused and broken up with other choices.

Since many children lack the skills to participate effectively in speaking activities the authors have found it useful to spend a whole day practising oral skills through the structures needed for differentiation by organisation. For instance, there could be a day on exploring the differences between two world religions through groupwork, where very little writing takes place.

8. Record and keep evidence of children's learning

There is a distinction to be made between assessment and the monitoring of children's progress. To monitor the children's progress the teacher needs to assess all the children on the same activity at the end of the topic. The results of these assessments then inform the reporting.

If teacher planning incorporates this distinction between assessment tasks and review for learning objectives then the assessment recording sheet need only show the key skills, knowledge, understanding and concepts that were prioritised and assessed through the end of topic assessment task. They need not show each individual learning objective.

Summate assessment should not be undertaken at the end of a year but periodically throughout the year. This involves specific assessment tasks for individual children designed to examine their progress on a selection of specific learning objectives that were planned. They can also be used to inform for records and reports to parents.

In our view teachers are responsible for monitoring their input of the curriculum and its effects and for planning, making judgements against planned criteria and recording assessments. However, that which many teachers describe as 'ongoing continuous assessment' of all the children's learning we regard as the children's responsibility. This then becomes the children monitoring their own progress and fits in with the ideas of self assessment, working to previous best and setting your own targets, all of which are outlined in the subsequent chapters.

We believe that children can be taught to do this monitoring and in our experience they have proved themselves to be extremely capable of marking their own and each other's work, giving accurate feedback on areas of strength and weakness, and setting targets for the next step needed to ensure development. Alongside the teacher's end-of-topic results there could therefore be a selection of work that the child has chosen as being their best, based upon criteria already shared with the teacher and their peers. We have found it useful for children to note on the work what it is they believe this work shows that they can do as a way of identifying the criteria that it demonstrates.

Whereas the teacher will only be able to manage to assess against prioritised criteria through specific planned tasks, children are able to make judgements against the full range of criteria if these are shared with them. The criteria are simply taken from the planning sheets where the planned learning objectives are recorded. Sometimes these may need to be put into 'child speak' but in our experience this is rarely needed as the children can be taught what the 'adult speak' means. For example, 'used phonic clues in reading' could be 'sounds out the words' or teachers could explain that the word 'phonic' means 'using the letter sounds' in the same way that teachers would explain that the proper word for water going into the atmosphere is evaporation. The resulting criteria can be shown as 'I can' statements, for example, 'I can use phonics clues to help when I am reading.'

These 'I can' sheets are a result of the process of sharing the criteria and the review of the children's learning against these criteria. For example, children in paired reading can record the number of times their partner uses a phonic cue to decode a word which is unfamiliar, then they can note the word and /or keep a tally of the number of times this is done. One very effective way of doing this, as well as for other aspects of reading, is to teach children to fill in a running record sheet as in the Key Stage 1 SATs. This record of a child's use of phonics can be kept by the child and will contribute to the child's understanding and ability to use phonics in their reading.

If the teacher is working in the ways outlined in this book then an individual child's record could contain the following:

- The observation schedules, peer records of their partners learning, peer assessment sheets (such as the running record in reading) and target setting records.
- The 'I can' sheets, for both skills training and curriculum content. These provide a summary of what the children can do. The day-to-day assessment of how near they are to meeting the criteria remains in the children's work folders.
- The teacher's record, based upon the assessment tasks set at the end of particular topics. Teachers may wish where appropriate to include the actual tasks as evidence alongside the record of their judgement about levels reached.
- Samples of work, annotated by the children, not only with the date and context, but also with the criterion that it demonstrates. This provides an excellent bank of evidence on which teachers can make summary reports to parents and to other teachers at transfer to other classes.

Children's individual records will therefore contain the result of the assessment based on the assessment tasks. A summary of the learning objectives planned for each year can form the record sheet for the individual child. This will relate to but not be constrained by the entire National Curriculum targets. Recording assessment is then very easy to manage as each assessment task will relate specifically to the recording sheet with no irrelevant or out of date information cluttering it up. This type of individual recording sheet can be taken directly from the planning sheet for the year which should contain:

- learning objectives;
- assessment tasks;
- criteria for making judgements about the quality of the work.

The authors visualise the skills training planning as taking place in parallel with, connected to and in relation with the curriculum planning. Ideally there should be a whole school plan to map the skills acquisition for all the children throughout their primary career. The skills training programme then should be planned, monitored and evaluated to ensure that the children receive systematic instruction in the skills they need to communicate and help one another effectively.

Those children who already have good communication skills should be encouraged to become models and then rewarded for being teachers and tutors of these skills. The authors have found that those children who struggle with writing or demonstrate poor or disruptive behaviour can be taught to highlight the positive communication skills they already possess and can tutor those who are perceived as very bright or even gifted in reading, writing or other academic subjects but who lack these listening and group-skills. In this way it is possible to find a strength that those with low self-esteem possess and reward and encourage them for it.

Monitoring and evaluation

Monitoring of the curriculum should be the random selection of the work of some of the children, preferably across the ability range, and across the time of the work. This random selection of children's work should be compared to the aims of the curriculum and should be used to help the teacher review their planning and delivery and replan for next time. It is a way of checking to see if what was intended to happen actually happened. In other words the curriculum delivery is constantly being monitored for effectiveness in terms of children's learning.

What teachers formerly saw as 'ongoing assessment' is actually useful for monitoring the curriculum. This is monitoring and evaluating the teaching of the curriculum and is not assessing individual children. To do this teachers need to have identified clearly in their planning what it is they are intending to teach both in terms of skills and content (knowledge and understanding).

Summary

As teachers become more skilled at:

- identifying the learning objectives;
- finding out what children know at the beginning of a topic so that they can help them to measure their own progress in learning (baseline assessment);
- trying out new teaching strategies and techniques;
- monitoring these techniques by recording the children's responses and the quality of work produced as the topic progresses;
- evaluating the techniques by comparing results of children's work – including assessment activity scores and rates of improvement with results from work taught another way;

so teachers will become researchers in their own classrooms and schools. This kind of research, the authors have found, empowers teachers. Teachers start to feel:

- more in control – they can see what is happening in the teaching and learning process;
- more optimistic – they can see the there really are 'other ways' for children to learn and these ways work;
- more pro-active – they can make decisions and prioritise both curriculum content and curriculum delivery in a more focused and precise way, justifying both with a rationale underpinned by a clear understanding of the teaching and learning process.

Chapter 4

Differentiation by Outcome

Traditionally, 'Differentiation by Outcome' is regarded by teachers as an open-ended task that is given to all children. The children then attempt this task in their own way and at their own pace, thus allowing for varieties in learning styles and abilities. A common example is the worksheet approach where teachers give the whole class the same worksheet and expect some children to complete it well, some to manage to complete it and others to do just a part of the work. The result of this is that all reach different learning outcomes. For instance, if a comprehension sheet is given to a class, those who complete just one question, those who complete five and those who complete ten questions have all gained different amounts of knowledge from the set piece. What teachers tend to do to overcome this is to adjust the difficulty of questions with the easier questions at the beginning getting harder as they go through. Assessment exercises such as SATs are in this format.

Teachers we have worked with have told us that this form of differentiation is problematic for the following reasons:

- it can lead to different learning outcomes for the children;
- this can create difficulties for assessment and recording;
- it causes classroom management difficulties, for example the difficulty of starting off the next lesson when children have all reached different points;
- it sets up tensions between the children as some progress more quickly than others: those who are ahead can feel resentful that they are always doing more work and sometimes ridicule those who are not as far on;
- those who are not as far on can get increasingly demoralised.

Teachers have also said to us that they often feel uncomfortable with this form of differentiation because they believe they have not taught anything to the more able children nor supported the weaker children. If they set a single task with no variation at all in the presentation for children of different aptitudes and abilities, and assess the outcomes, it does not seem fair to the children.

The authors have come to the conclusion that it is the inclusion of writing in every task that may be responsible for limiting a child's learning. For many children writing is difficult, it is not the way that they would choose to record their learning and for them writing down what they have seen or done amounts to a punishment and restricts the amount they can say. For example one child with specific learning difficulties described a story orally to his support teacher. When he came to write this story he wrote the phrase 'big lorry' and when asked why he had not used the word 'articulated' which was the word he had used orally, he said it was because he could not write 'articulated'. The class teacher was then unaware of the child's vocabulary and possible knowledge of lorries. In the experience of the authors it is this difficulty with one form of recording, i.e. writing, which can actually create learning difficulties. In this sense Special Needs are created by the writing task.

Some teachers fear that if children who are not very good at writing are not 'made to practise' writing then they will never improve. We have found that an interesting paradox occurs. In classrooms where our model of Differentiation by Outcome is used, gradually, over a period of time, those children who initially avoided writing begin to include some writing alongside the more practical methods of recording. They may always prefer a practical method for day to day learning and recording but they will have the skills and confidence to be able to use the more formal style when occasionally required. We have noticed many adults doing the same thing. Problems with writing can also be addressed individually and separately through Differentiation by Paired Task.

The recognition that some children can demonstrate their knowledge, understanding and skills through oracy and practical activities but fail in the written tasks, has led us to the model for learning outlined previously. This same understanding is the basis of our Differentiation by Outcome theory. This form of differentiation is a complex area because there are many variations possible, and teachers are often unaware of the many options. These are the variables of Stimulus, Task and Recording. The grid (Figure 4.1) illustrates this model. Once a teacher has understood the principles on which the model is based then these can be applied to any part of the National Curriculum. The principles are:

- the stimuli or input can be varied,
- there are ways in which a variety of tasks can be offered, and
- alternative methods of recording can be encouraged.

In the following section we will explore the different elements which can be varied in order to structure a lesson to provide learning, not just assessment, through differentiating by outcome.

Variety of stimuli

The variety of stimuli can consist of a mixture of artefacts or information sources available around the classroom from which the children can select so that each child receives a different input of information

Differentiation by outcome
(different product - same learning objectives)

1. Varied stimuli	Varied task	Varied recording
2. Common stimuli	Varied task	Varied recording
3. Varied stimuli	Common task	Varied recording
4. Common stimuli	Common task	Varied recording
5. Common stimuli	Common task	Common recording

Figure 4.1 Grid illustrating stimulus, task, recording model.

even though the main topic covered will remain the same. A library collection of reference books will cover the same topic in a variety of ways and at a variety of levels. In our experience it is not necessary for the teacher to guide children to particular books that they feel are at an appropriate reading level as children are able to gather information from books that are at a much higher reading level through referring to pictures and captions. Teachers should, however, pay attention to teaching children about using an index and contents page to find the appropriate information. Yellow post-it stickers can help to make finding sections of the book easier.

Alternatively the stimulus can be a variety of different inputs given to the whole class e.g. video, presentation by outside speaker, teachers or children with knowledge or expertise in the field. Also possible is the presentation of information from books, posters and artefacts to the whole class. This ensures that the whole class has access to the wide range of information prior to their choosing one aspect which they wish to record or investigate further. This can be reassuring for children who may find differentiation by outcome challenging to their present level of independence.

Access to the wider picture first can help children select intelligently an aspect in which they are interested whilst seeing where it fits into the topic. Whole class topic webs, created with or by the children, based upon the variety of information sources available, can help children locate their own special study and see the links between their work and others.

Even quite young children can be involved in topic planning. For example one teacher we know organised her Year One children into groups of four to brainstorm the topic 'shops'. Each group had a large sheet of paper and an adult who had been briefed to be a scribe and encourager of all children participating but not an ideas provider or ideas sorter. The result of this activity was the discovery by the teacher that the children were most interested in 'who was allowed to go to the shops on their own and when.' This would not have been included in the topic if the teacher had planned it by herself. It led to some interesting work on surveys, and bar charts as well as discussion about safety.

Too often the planning aspect of the topic is kept by the teacher who reveals aspects of the topic one by one in an effort to tantalise the children into interest or to prevent children being overwhelmed by the quantity of work involved in a topic. The result unfortunately is that children do not make links between different aspects of a topic and don't therefore get a clear conceptual understanding. If the planning is shared with the children then they can contribute to the resources for variety of stimulus. It is important to tell children in advance what the topics are and that materials will be needed for models. Our experience is that when we do they often bring in extra information such as books and leaflets from visits.

Variety of task

Often we give all the children the same task but the task itself is open-ended. This is known as a common task. The way in which the task is undertaken is not prescribed, indeed the teacher strives to acknowledge and present many different, alternative ways of carrying out the task so that children understand that all are equally valid. This can only be achieved if the teacher is clear about the actual learning objective of the lesson and understands that the method of recording the knowledge gained is not important and should never limit the child's ability to be successful in demonstrating what he or she has learned.

A variety of task is also known as a workshop/circus/roundabout as described above. In our experience children formerly labelled as having a short concentration span because they so rarely complete the simplest of tasks, start to demonstrate their ability to concentrate for long periods when working in their preferred style. This enables the teacher to see what methods are best suited to particular children; very often the teacher is pleasantly surprised by the achievement and ability of children who have otherwise not been able to show this.

The children need to be encouraged to complete the learning objective in their own ways.

Variety of recording

Children should be encouraged to use as many different ways of recording information as possible. These include: flow diagrams, note taking, mind maps, cartoons, key word lists, tracings, drawings, charts, models, videos, audio tapes, photographs, validation and witness statements. These should be openly discussed as possibilities and teachers should avoid anyone making value judgements about children using 'easy' methods. The variety of products allows interesting and stimulating displays that children can use to inform each other of their own particular findings.

Some teachers say that if the children are allowed to record in any way they like then the teachers will not have the kind of evidence needed for inspection and reporting to parents. This is a concern about evidence. For learning purposes we feel that it is essential that a variety of recording is always offered so that children who find writing difficult do not have their learning growth stunted. Hence the reason for including variety of recording in every column of the grid.

However, we recognise the fact that children may well need to use a particular form of recording, usually writing, when they carry out an assessment task and it for this reason that we feel learning objectives and assessment activities should be separated and their different requirements clearly explained to children.

There are, however, many ways in which evidence can be recorded apart from writing. Many teachers know this already because they have started to collect evidence of children's achievements for the initiatives in Records of Achievement. Some of the ways in which evidence of learning and progress can be collected include the following:

- A verbal review can be recorded by a peer when children are discussing their learning in pairs.
- Another adult in the classroom or an older age child can act as scribe in a learning circle.
- The children can be asked to provide annotated drawings of things they have made to go in their record folder.
- Teachers can provide children with sheets with learning objectives on them and children can draw or put in cartoon or flow chart their progress towards these objectives.

Drafts are evidence of learning and progression also. If the teacher encourages drafting and redrafting then these stages in the child's progress can be kept as evidence. For example, in one classroom where such exploration and refinement through practice was emphasised, Year Three and Four children often chose to re-do worksheets made available during wet play times or choosing times. They would then choose to add these work sheets to their work folders, sometimes replacing the previous worksheet. We feel it is important that the teacher encourages children to do this so that the idea of draft and redraft becomes natural. The final piece is also evidence of learning.

Differentiation by Outcome can be a useful way of structuring an activity for assessment when assessment is the focus. For example, at the end of a History topic on the Romans you may well ask the children to write a description of life in a Roman town. You would remind them that they will get marks for details they give about aspects of life such as: food, clothes, houses, daily routines, and that they will get a mark for each time they say how we know. The children are set a common task, they have common stimuli and they will all write an account so it has a common recording system. These children would have been told from the outset of their topic that this would be the assessment activity and they could have been preparing for it during the 'learning' time. This type of differentiation can also be used as a base line assessment. For example in PE you might show the children what you mean by dribbling a ball and ask the children to dribble a ball up and down the room moving around each other. You would then have the opportunity to watch the children and assess who has good dribbling skills and who has little control over the ball. This would allow you next to teach the skill in an appropriate way, either to the whole class, or by using 'mixed dribbling ability pairs' or 'same dribbling ability' pairs.

Learning objective and learning outcomes

Using this approach to Differentiation by Outcome the children all reach the same learning objective. It is only the product, the way in which the children do and record the task that is different. In this approach the 'outcome' which is differentiated is the product. One consequence of differentiating in this way is that the issue of low expectations which has been identified by both HMI and OFSTED and outlined in Chapter 1 is dealt with. With this model of Differentiation by Outcome the teacher expects all children to reach and achieve the learning objective regardless of ability, strengths or weakness. Children's individual differences are noted, catered for and taken into account by offering the variety of recording and choice of task. However, the teacher has high expectations of children, the teacher believes in children, in both their prior knowledge and in their potential to build on that knowledge. Differentiation by Outcome in this model is not about tolerating different levels of achievement in terms of knowledge and understanding, or tolerating different standards. It is an approach which expects, demands and gets high standards from all children regardless of their ability but it builds in structures that are designed to support children as they learn in order to help them reach this high standard.

The key to using differentiation by outcome is understanding the distinction between the learning outcome and the learning objective. The learning outcome is the product that is determined by the way the child chooses to record and present their learning. The learning objective is the knowledge, skills or understanding that the child is to acquire.

So it is possible for children to record in different ways but still demonstrate their learning in relation to the same learning outcome. If, for example, the objective is for the children to become familiar with life in the cities for the poor in Victorian England then the learning objective for the children will be to demonstrate their knowledge and understanding of this subject. The children may choose to demonstrate their knowledge through cartoons, drawing, drama, tape, video of drama, poster or writing a factual account. In this way the variety of recording produces a variety of products but the learning objective and learning outcome are the same for all the children in the class.

So in our model there are three main components:

- a variety of stimuli – not just written material;
- choice for the children in the way they carry out the task;
- choice in the way they record their learning – this difference in recording leads to different products.

The challenge for many teachers is to define the learning objective and to separate this from the task. We have found that this is not easy because it is not the way we have been trained to teach. To move away from thinking of the task to thinking of the learning is a new way of teaching and is demanding, but in our experience is worthwhile. The most important part of this idea of a learning objective is that it is expressed in phrases that the child can understand and in such a way that a child can demonstrate it. Knowing and understanding need to be expressed in concrete terms. For example: 'by the end of this lesson you should be able to tell me three objects that float and three that sink,' or 'by the end of this lesson you should be able to tell me which of these three things you think will float and which will sink and give me a reason based on the experiments we did last lesson.' This form of learning objective may differ considerably from the objectives previously written into teachers' lesson plans.

Sometimes involving the children in the brainstorming part of the lesson planning helps teachers to be concrete and explicit about the learning objectives. The clearer the learning objectives are to the children the more likely they will be able to demonstrate success in their efforts to achieve them and the more responsibility the children can take for their own learning. Thus learning objectives and independent learners go together.

Differentiation by outcome supporting independent learning

We have found that many teachers have coped with the introduction and constraints of the National Curriculum by having the whole class doing the same task at the same time. In this way they feel that they can control the curriculum and compile evidence for assessment more easily. Many teachers feel uncomfortable with this way of teaching but know of no alternative which will ensure evidence that all the children have covered an area of knowledge as is their entitlement. The differentiation by outcome activities described in this chapter and in Appendix 1 show how all children can be engaged in activities to increase their knowledge and understanding around the strands of the National Curriculum which the teacher has selected whilst at the same time being free to choose an approach to the task which suits their learning style.

Whilst most teachers accept the principles outlined in this chapter they do feel uneasy about several factors. These include:

- pupil choice;
- consultation with children on preferred leaning styles;
- children having ownership.

We acknowledge teachers' unease but have found that all these lead to pupils developing a sense of personal responsibility and enable them to become independent learners.

Pupil choice

In order to help pupil choice the tasks should be carefully thought out and planned to allow equal success for all children in completing the task even if they demonstrate different levels of skills, knowledge and conceptual understanding. The rationale for pupil choice is to do with accommodating different learning styles and maintaining motivation.

When there was a lack of choice and the task was rigidly prescribed it was not just children with learning difficulties who struggled. Some children rarely completed task because they could not do the writing; others didn't because they were detailed and methodical workers and therefore there was never enough time for them. Yet others, usually quite capable children, learned not to finish the task because finishing meant being presented with extra work. Any of these incidents can lead to disruptive behaviour.

A way of offering structured choice is the organisation of mini workshops or a roundabout or circus of activities. In this 'circus' or 'workshop' arrangement there are different tables with different activities. These activities can be closed or very open-ended. A closed task may be a simple set of instructions such as the directions to make a Roman stylus and wax tablet. An open-ended task may be building a tower of newspaper to support the weight of a book. Children can then choose to move around the tables doing all the activities in an order of their choosing or to do one activity in more detail. A teacher we met recently told us that he found that children work much more quickly on problem solving tasks when he structures his workstations so that there are six children at every workstation. When it is time to change activities and move on to new workstations, three children stay at the station they have just been at and three move on. The three staying then tutor the newly arrived ones. These tutors who have stayed are the three to move on next time and become tutees at the next station. He is delighted with the difference this change in structure makes to children's learning and speed with which they complete the circus.

Initially children may be unable to choose effectively. The reason for this is that they have been used to the teacher setting the task for them and find the offer of choice so contrary to their previous expectations, experiences and ways of working that they exhibit poor behaviour. This can be rectified by establishing rules for moving on from one activity to another. These may include:

- Children being asked to finish one activity before moving on or they might be asked to move on after a certain time period. Timers are useful to establish fairness in this case.
- Defining the number of children that can be at one table at once, freeing children to move around when they wish but preventing a chaotic number of children at any one activity.

- Defining a 'finished' activity so that the rule about moving on when you have finished means that the teacher has a say in whether the product is finished or not.
- Requiring the children to carry out a minimum-maximum number of activities. This encourages children to manage their time effectively.

Teachers are anxious that if the children are left to choose for themselves they will never do anything. Our own experience of offering choice to children and observing them in these situations is the reverse of this. Children seem to actually do more work and produce more in these choosing situations rather than less. It seems to us that the choice is motivating and that it is the lack of choice and the type of activity that is usually presented to children that causes the present difficulty.

Listening to children in the Early Years base has convinced the authors of the value that children place on choosing and therefore of the importance in utilising it in the learning process. This does not mean that 'choosing time' as a reward should be stopped but that children should be given a choice about the way they approach their 'work' and thus be enabled to reach the learning objective as well as having the highly prized reward of 'choosing time.'

It is important that children are allowed to work in the way in which they find learning easiest because then they will achieve. Although this may sound obvious our observations of primary school practice demonstrate that this is rarely happening. Teachers interpret 'offering a variety of learning styles' as offering a variety of activities throughout the week. This is not sufficient. Children need a method of learning which suits them for each activity. If teachers had to try to match each child to an activity which incorporated their preferred learning style, teaching would be totally impossible. We believe that the way forward is for teachers to consult with children.

This does not have to be one to one consultations but can be achieved through:

- learning circles where children talk about ways in which they learn best;
- paired discussion on learning strategies for a particular task;
- small group sharing on how you achieved your task as well as feedback on the task itself;
- teachers initiating possible ways to approach a task whilst leaving the choice to the children.

These can establish the classroom 'norm' that there is no one way of doing things. We all approach things slightly differently, some very differently, and I may be able to learn something by listening to the way that others do things and then incorporating it into my own approach.

Teachers are concerned that consulting with children will both take too long and produce so many options that the classroom and

Consulting with children on preferred learning styles

curriculum planning will be chaotic. This would be true if the teacher had to organise every different activity chosen and provide the task. However, our experience is that when children are consulted about the way in which they are going to approach the learning and demonstrate that they have achieved the learning objective, they are more than capable of organising themselves. In fact the range of activities and variety of products will not result in chaos, it will simply mean that the children successfully complete their task more independently.

The children who like to work quickly and do practical things such as models, masks and solutions using technology can make several things during the time span. Children who like to work slowly and methodically in detail can do so on one project. Children who aren't sure and like structure can keep to the suggestions of the teacher. In this way different learning styles are all catered for and with practice the teacher can learn to provide a time-frame which is realistic and the children can learn to keep to it. It is important that the learning objective is stated and displayed clearly for the children and that they are reminded of it at frequent points. The children will also learn that there are several ways of reaching the same end point, giving them further choices for tackling their next learning objective.

If the children initially have difficulties in deciding how to plan their own learning activities then they can be encouraged by the teacher to consult with another child about possible ways to do this. Some teachers fear that the children who have always needed help and support in the past will flounder in situations where there is choice. In fact we have found that in time these children seem to respond very well to this form of differentiation. We account for this in the following way. Many children with learning difficulties struggle with reading and writing. In schools where there is an emphasis on writing as the main form of recording and reading as the main way to acquire knowledge and information about all subjects, the children both notice this and evaluate themselves according to this criterion. They may actually say in circle-time 'I am no good at reading/writing.' By the end of the Keystage One these self evaluations rapidly convert to 'I am no good at school work.' Given the absence of sand, water and 'choosing time' in Year Three and the clear predominance of writing and reading to access the science, history, geography and technology curriculum, we feel this is a fairly accurate assessment. However, rather than seeing a less able child's preference for play and practical activities as a sign of poor overall ability we see it as a preferred learning style which, if it can be harnessed for learning, will help the child to reveal what they really do know and build on that knowledge in their own way.

What usually happens in Year Three however is that the child is provided with adult support to help them complete their written work and carry out the numerous reading tasks which are the only gateway to other subjects. Learned helplessness can then be seen to set in. Children gradually become more and more dependent on their adult helper and do not even get their own books out or write the date until prompted. In the 'choice' situation if children have already developed such learned helplessness they can be encouraged to work together with a partner of similar ability until they gradually regain confidence to work alone. In our experience these children do slowly gain confidence as a result of completing tasks in their own way and in their own time. What is crucial, however, is teacher and peer approval for their efforts. The more their sense of self-worth is restored the more their confidence increases until gradually they are clearly getting more tasks done. For these children too the ability and willingness to practice the skills they need for their areas of weakness increases.

A strong sense of self-worth and self-value seems to be crucial for any of us to be prepared to look at weaknesses as a target setting area. This increase in self-worth can also come from the sharing of 'ways in which we do things,' discussion at the end of the lesson. What less able children learn from such discussions is that there are lots of ways to do things, there is a variety of ways in which we can record, they are all of equal value but some are more appropriate to certain situations and some are required in certain assessment situations. This is a very different perspective to 'I am no good' and is the hallmark of an independent learner.

Children having ownership

Whilst teachers would agree that they want their children to be independent learners and to have ownership of their own learning they are sometimes anxious about their own role if they organise the children into activities where they make their own choices. In practice, however, teachers find that their role is a new one but one that they welcome. It is one of teaching as opposed to managing or disciplining or resource allocating. In fact we find that teachers who try out this and other ways of differentiating say to us, 'This is what I always thought teaching could be, now I can really teach and help the children to learn.' What happens of course is that the more the children organise themselves and each other the less class organisation the teacher has to do and the more teaching they can do.

The role of the teacher here is twofold. It is both that of facilitator, ensuring the smooth running of the workshops or activities and also that of tutor; the teacher can go round and offer advice and support with the models and technology projects; they can sit at a table and engage the children working on a play in a discussion about play and drama formats.

The teacher can and should also observe, preferably using a recording sheet. This means that she can provide pupil feedback, both 'academic' feedback and 'working together' feedback. In this situation where there is: supportive peer feedback, teacher feedback and pupil self assessment then children who behave in ways that upset other children gradually come to hear and accept the difference between their own self perceptions and the perceptions of others in the group, including the teacher. It is in these circumstances that the child is more likely to make a commitment to change their behaviour.

The teacher's role is also to praise and value the differences between children when they talk about the different ways in which they approach a task and learn from a task. The teacher needs to constantly value difference rather than valuing conformity. It is the teacher's job therefore to structure peer feedback so that all the children become increasingly aware of who is good at what based on what they have seen each other do.

There is a concern in offering choice that children won't do their own work but will all copy from each other. Whilst this may be true for some of the less able children in the initial stages of this kind of work in fact the opposite is true for the majority of children. The copying amongst the least able should not be seen as a problem initially but a stage that they are going through on their journey from learned helplessness to independence and ownership. Indeed copying the best method demonstrates that they are beginning to make good choices about learning. The children are initiating activities and not just sitting and waiting for an adult to 'come and do it for them.' For many children the 'choice' leads to some very creative work indeed. Their freedom to try out new approaches may mean that they come up with ideas that the teacher has never considered before. Sometimes the 'off the wall' method (which is actually creativity) is the one which is most appropriate for the situation.

In classrooms where differentiation by outcome with a range of choice is the norm we have observed children choosing one method of approaching a task, having difficulty with that approach and then going on to choose another method, often one they have observed another child using successfully. Teachers need to openly encourage this adaptation of other children's methods. For example the child who has used the method originally can be asked by the teacher to explain what they did to those interested in using it. The teacher can praise the one who has gone on to try another method; this is a crucial way of helping children to maintain motivation and a sense of self-worth. It teaches them a longterm strategy which is of relevance in the every day world, i.e. if one approach doesn't work, try another; it also encourages the children to increase their range of learning styles.

Summary

One of the main advantages of Differentiating by Outcome in this way of organising teaching and learning is that more children actually 'do their work.' It is this sense of achievement of completed tasks that enables children to feel confident and begin to identify their own learning style and their strengths, and become increasingly independent learners. Through this process they can become skilled enough to start to devise tasks for themselves. The tasks they set for themselves are designed to: reach a learning objective, or to demonstrate knowledge they have. See Appendix 1 for examples from the National Curriculum which illustrate this approach to Differentiation by Outcome.

Chapter 5

Differentiation by Paired Task

The authors have stated that for them Differentiation is about all children having entitlement and access to the curriculum. It is often assumed that mixed ability will mean that the 'bright' children will need individual work to stretch them, the average children will not need much individual work and the 'slow children' will need a 'remedial' form of individual work which is both simple enough to provide success and repetitive enough to provide the child with practice of the 'basics.' The authors' concerns about such an approach are to do with the focus on children's differences, and the fact that the solution is provided by the teacher. In the authors' experiences these two factors very often result in dependency by the child on an adult and also in ridiculing by peers. Additionally children who get help from adult support teachers may well attribute success to the adult and not to themselves. In the authors' experience the assumptions teachers make about ability also result in children being limited and held back. The authors have observed that this limiting of children takes place when learning, assessment and remediation are delivered through one task. This is often called differentiation by task and this approach is illustrated in Figure 5.1.

For example, a common way to teach a History topic is for the teacher to tell the children a story, then give them a cloze exercise to fill in which is subsequently marked. The children who have difficulties in writing will probably be given an easier sheet possibly with key words written at the end. In this situation the child has had no opportunity to learn the History component of the lesson or to rehearse their learning of the History or to practice their area of weakness, which is writing. Instead the children are being asked to learn through their area of weakness which is writing, and in order to help them cope with the writing they are given simplified history which may not be their area of weakness. In a short space of time the child who was either open minded about history or who was keen on history will come to dislike it because of the method of learning. When quizzed about this insistence on teaching the subject through

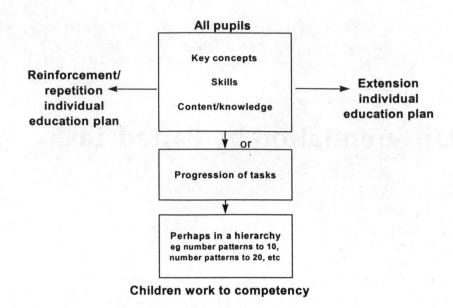

Figure 5.1 Differentiation by task: old way.

reading and writing (the areas of weakness for many children, including bright children) teachers will say it is because the children have to write for assessment purposes. Whilst the authors accept the fact that children will indeed need to write for the assessment activity they see it as important to separate out learning the subject from the practice in the area of difficulty, for example, writing. The previous chapter and the next chapter highlight ways in which this separation of learning can take place.

When the teacher and the child focus on the child's area of difficulty it is helpful to use target setting to make progress:
- possible
- manageable
- observable
- rewardable.

Such good practice is outlined in the Special Needs Code of Practice in the reference to Individual Education Programmes.

Individual Target Setting (IEPs) – a framework for differentiating

The concern that all teachers have in working with Individual Education Programmes is the time it takes both to write out the programmes and to ensure that they are carried out. Indeed, in our experience, this is the driving force behind the requests from mainstream teachers for support for children with special needs. What has not yet emerged in the literature is the difficulty that most teachers have, whether they are specialist or not, in getting the children to make any progress with their IEPs after the teachers have written them. If the child does not make progress on their IEP there tends to be an assumption that there is something wrong with the child. For example, if a child has been identified as having a specific learning difficulty with reading and he or she fails to make progress with their IEP, the assumption is that the child has a more widespread learning difficulty.

Our own experience as adults tells us that working to a target is very hard. This is borne out time and again by the medical profession who despair of their patients because they fail to keep to the targets set by their GP for weight loss or for giving up smoking. The authors note that the slimming clubs who work on both rewards and peer support usually have more success than GPs. We have observed that children need the same: peer support and rewards to help them make progress with these very hard targets. We believe that setting targets and achieving those targets is difficult because of the negative feelings of low self-worth that we all have about our area of weakness and failure. What most of us prefer to do is to forget about or *not* think about or focus on such areas.

Presently only children identified as having special needs are working with targets on IEPs. Our own research evidence shows that children with special needs have low self-esteem and they already feel different; therefore, for many children, the process of having a different curriculum in the shape of individual targets simply underscores the difference and increases their sense of low self-worth. In many cases low self-worth and low academic achievement go hand in hand so low self-worth and not achieving on the small steps targets is also quite likely. For the authors then, the way forward is in taking away the sense of being different.

An improved approach would be for children to be in a group where *everybody* is working towards a target, where *everyone* has the opportunity to be helper and *everyone* the opportunity to be helped. For most teachers there is an expectation that this help will come from an additional adult and the frustration for teachers is that this expectation is thwarted by a lack of resources. The form that would be useful for the organisation of IEPs for all in the classroom is illustrated in Figure 5.2.

In this chapter we ask teachers to consider the possibility of using the peer group to help each other as well as the adults who are available. In our experience children's differences are not only seen as a classroom management and resources problem by the teacher, the children too see other children who are different as a problem. As with teachers, this difficulty with difference applies to children at both ends of the ability spectrum. For instance if a child appears bright the peer group will typically:

- label the child as abnormal;
- call them names such as 'boff' 'keener';
- not pick that child for the sports activities;
- not invite them to join games in the playground.

Putting an adult helper in to work with the brighter or less able child highlights the difference and confirms their separateness. This leads to constant and high levels of negative feedback from the peer group and so any positive effects of the extra help are undermined by the consequent fall in self-esteem. This issue is addressed through Differentiation by Paired Task.

I E P
Individual Education Plan

date.........................

Child's name.....................................
Teacher's name................................

I will be able to / I will
Teaching objective(s)

by
time span

to do this we will have to
resources, personnel, time

the check will be
assessment

my reward will be / the result will be
reinforcement / outcome

signed ....(child)

....(teacher)

achieved ....(date)

Figure 5.2   Form of IEPs for all children (© Helen Newton).

Differentiation by Paired Task

Differentiation by Paired Task is based upon the premise that children, because they have different strengths and different ways of learning as well as different weaknesses, can help each other both with their weaknesses and their strengths so that *all* children are working to improvement.

As stated, the authors have found that the children achieve more when learning and assessment are separated, so that everyone learns together using whatever strategy suits their learning style. Having separated learning from assessment the teacher is then faced with the difficulty of helping children to improve their area of weakness for the assessment.

The assessment activity, for either the learning objective or the end of topic assessment, may highlight aspects of work that children either find difficult or could improve on. We recommend that teachers establish a norm in their classroom based on the model introduced by Tim Brighouse of Birmingham Education Authority: 'Improving on Previous Best.' If all children are encouraged to look at their assessment results, target set for improvement with their teacher and work towards improvement on their Previous Best then there is no difference between the child who is practising his spelling of 'what, when and where' and the child who is trying to improve his inclusion of referenced material with appropriate quotations instead of importing chunks of a multi media Encyclopaedia. Both children are working on improvement.

The authors recognise that work towards improvement on Previous Best is usefully achieved by working towards specific targets and in that respect the authors endorse the ideas of Individual Education Programmes brought in by the Code of Practice. However the authors believe that this target setting should be for all children and should be carried out in peer tutoring pairs not individually. We call this Differentiation by Paired Task. (See Figure 5.3.)

The advantages of Differentiation by Paired Task are that it:

- enables children to feel the same as everyone else through whole class sessions on target setting;
- stops 'put downs' and ridiculing because children start to help one another, share their fears and anxieties, and come to know each other as learners;
- ensures that children get one to one help in their area of weakness;
- enables children to feel supported when working on their area of weakness;
- means that the child is more likely to reach their target and make genuine improvement because they get help on the way in which they will approach their target from someone who has fairly recently learned this target themselves;
- means that any success the child does make is likely to be attributed to themselves and their effort and not to an adult.

It is our view that structures must be introduced to enable Differentiation by Paired Task to happen. The purpose of the structures is to

Work in pairs to:

Complete a task	support (self-esteem) scaffolding (Bruner) clarification (Vygotsky)
Work together on one person's work, identify a problem. Break it into small steps	(peer tutoring IEP's for all)
Work together on one aspect of one step. One <u>teaches</u> the other	targeted peer tutoring individualised learning
Work together to set a target for the learning objective, and the assessed task	peer support self-esteem
Work together to consider how they learn	metacognition

Figure 5.3 Differentiation by paired task.

ensure that differences are explicitly recognised and used by children in order to help each other. This requires a change of focus for both teachers and children. The new focus involves a shift away from thinking about *differences in ability*, towards emphasising the *differences in the ways that we learn best*. It is also an emphasis away from *individuals working on their targets alone* towards *peer tutoring support for target setting*.

This change of focus for the teacher means that instead of seeing the differences between children as a problem requiring 'extra' (extra planning, worksheets, tasks) the teacher can begin to see the difference as a resource to be built on. The teacher can start to match children's strengths and weaknesses with each other instead of matching the child to the task perceived by the teacher to be most appropriate. Once teachers start working with Differentiation by Paired Task they find that instead of thinking: 'Oh, I've got all these different abilities. How can I get them all to work separately at their own level and in line with the scheme of work?' they start to think: 'Oh good, I've got one child with dyslexia with a wide general knowledge and a good attitude to work, and another child who has learning difficulties and as a result is "switched off" from learning and school, so I can pair them up.'

In summary, what the teacher is using through Differentiation by Paired Task is the pupils' ability to help each other and the benefits of difference:

- different abilities;
- different knowledge;
- different strengths and skills.

This will mean that rather than having different spelling groups according to ability in spelling the children will be paired to talk about how they learn spellings.

What will be revealed is a wide variety of systems for learning such as repeating out loud the letters over and over, writing them down in a list, writing the same word out over and over again, making up a song, repeating with a skipping rope in rhythm, writing the letters in the air, saying the letters as you flick into a handstand, coloured boxes around words to highlight them. This approach can, of course, be used within similar ability spelling groups.

For us these different methods correspond to the Multiple Intelligence idea put forward by Howard Gardner (1993), so it is not surprising that there is this variety of methods which include bodily kinaesthetic ones. It then becomes clear that whilst the 'look, cover, write, check' method for learning spellings will suit some children who would choose to learn through lists or writing out, it is of little help to those who learn in a rhythmic or kinaesthetic way.

Very often special needs support teachers do discover a child's preferred learning style and so are able to help them but this is usually after a great deal of time has been spent in trial and error, presenting work in as wide a variety of ways as they can think of in order to find the best match between strategy and child. Sometimes in this 'one to one' situation the children can be defensive and will not be able to identify how they learn as they are already under the pressure of knowing that they must indeed learn in a very different way from anyone else as they need extra help. With the whole class discussing their different approaches to learning it no longer becomes a stigma to be different.

Differentiation by Paired Task is target setting in an area of weakness and practising to improve in that area through being peer tutored rather than adult tutored. It focuses on being supported and getting one to one help, which is what most teachers say they want for their children.

Target setting and achieving those targets is very difficult for children. There are stages in the target setting process which are outlined below, which are far more easily reached when children receive help. There has been an expectation that this help should be provided by an adult. The resource implication for this is tremendous and can never be fulfilled. However, children can be helped to set targets by their peers, if the teacher structures them to do so, following the stages below. Children need to be taught to help each other with target setting by:

- helping to identify the problem;
- setting a broad target;
- setting a specific target;
- identifying a time scale and a reward;
- choosing a method of teaching and learning which suits the learner;
- spending time (in a one to one situation supporting learning that is most helpful);

Stages in setting and meeting targets

- assessing progress in a way chosen by the learner;
- rewarding success;
- reviewing to identify the problem and work towards changes in the method.

In addition to learning to help with target setting children need to be taught the skills of tutoring in order to be able to help their partner achieve the targets identified. The skills needed and the stages in which they should be taught are outlined later in this chapter.

Paired Task through the use of structured peer tutoring

We believe that children need to work collaboratively together to learn because they need the support of another person to take the risks that learning requires. This is laid out in chapter two. The collaboration we are referring to in this chapter is of a different nature however. It is explicit teaching or helping by one child for another. This means that children need to be taught the quite complex skills that they need to carry out these roles. To this extent teachers are right to be anxious. We cannot simply put children together and expect them either to help each other or to do this well. Teachers are also concerned about the role of the tutor in the peer tutoring situation, as it may appear that they are shirking their responsibilities by not helping the learning of the tutor. The benefits of peer tutoring to the tutor as well as the tutee are not always recognised by adults – parents and teachers alike. These are outlined below.

When one person teaches another then both gain from this interaction. The tutor gains because they need to clarify their thoughts, their understanding and their knowledge in order to teach it. This clarification process often leads to a better deeper understanding of the subject and can contribute to a conceptual understanding as most newly qualified teachers will testify. In fact the more the tutor has to work out what and how to teach something the more they are forced to clarify their own understanding and conceptual overview. This is probably because they are working in their 'zone of proximal development' (Vygotsky, 1962), with material that they are still unsure about as well as material they are sure of. In fact questions from the tutee often move tutors from the 'sure' to the 'unsure area' requiring the tutor to clarify this material for themselves as well as for the tutee. The research shows that although both partners increase their academic score it is the tutor who gains most. (Topping, 1988) This increase in academic score may also be because peer tutoring requires the tutor to focus on the way in which she learns, which is known as metacognition. It seems that children may begin to understand how they learn when they first try to teach something to someone else.

The tutor also gains because they feel helpful, needed, wanted and so have a positive evaluation of themselves. In fact peer tutoring improves the self-esteem of the tutor. In order that everyone in the classroom has the opportunity for enhanced self-esteem as a tutor and that the possible feelings of dependency for the tutee are diminished it is important that a variety of pairings are used and that teachers keep an open mind about pairings. Traditionally peer tutoring has been the pairing of the most able with the least able. In our view all children should have the opportunity to be a tutor and in particular, teachers should ensure that children with low self-esteem have the opportunity to be the tutor.

This means attending to a variety of pairings so that sometimes

- the most able are tutoring the least able;
- the least able are tutoring the most able;
- the least able are tutoring each other;
- the most able are tutoring each other.

To achieve this variety we recommend the use of both cross age tutoring and tutoring in as wide a range of subject areas as possible. Even the weakest children can tutor younger children, giving them that sense of worth and responsibility. Teachers are often surprised and delighted by the ability of the least able children to both diagnose the needs of younger children and come up with ideas for helping them. Some schools have even arranged inter-school activities, a school for moderate learning difficulties working with a school for severe learning difficulties for example on a drama project, in order to help the children with moderate learning difficulties feel they were needed. The same MLD school teamed up with a local primary school and in this situation the disaffected Year Six pupils 'helped' some of the autistic MLD children both in the classroom and the playground and verbally and visibly gained in their sense of self-worth as a result of these interactions.

The tutee gains similarly in two ways. They have increased time spent on the task and they experience increased success due to the ready availability of appropriate teaching where the explanations are at a level which is congruent with their own present level of thought. Thus there is support when and where it is needed, without recourse to the teacher. All these things contribute to the tutee being successful and vitally they are able to attribute their success to their own efforts. The advantages to both tutor and tutee are summarised below:

- The tutee gets individual tuition and high levels of attention.
- That stigma of not knowing, asking the teacher for help, being seen as ignorant, or 'can't do it' is taken away, so long as everyone in the class is at some point a tutee and not just the least able.
- The child gets help when they need it, when they are stuck and not when the teacher is free to help them. Many children get de-motivated or time fill by misbehaving whilst waiting for the teacher.
- The children who are the tutors often find alternative ways – words phrases or similes – to explain something, which can result in the tutee understanding something for the first time. For example one child we worked with, case study M, was a Year Three non-reader. Adults practised the 'sounding out' technique with him frequently, to no avail. R was teamed up with him for peer tutoring because R had just learned to read. After

several unsuccessful attempts to say the letters and get M to make the word, R used the phrase, 'C-A-T – CAT, M, listen, you just say the letters and sort of squish 'em together.' M looked in amazement and said 'Is that all reading is then, sayin' the letters an' squishin' 'em together?' His reading began in earnest that day as the adults rushed forward to say 'Yes darling, that's all reading is.'

- The children who are tutors are closer to the tutee because their memory of how they learned that knowledge or skill themselves is very fresh. They can therefore often see more clearly where the next step is for that child.

If the children do not work together then they are being set individual work in the belief that it will encourage their independence. Paradoxically it seems that when teachers set 'practice' work for children to encourage their independence it results in increased dependence by the children on the teacher's approval. This may be explained by the fact that when children are made to work individually, before they are ready, they feel vulnerable, exposed and anxious. What we often observe in Primary classrooms are children who have been set 'special work' for their targets working very slowly, checking every two minutes with the teacher saying 'Is this right?' or 'What shall I do now?' Whereas in fact, when challenged the children do know that the work is right and are perfectly aware of what to do next. This is an aspect of 'Learned Helplessness' (Seligman, 1978), and for us and most of the teachers we talk to it is the antithesis of independence.

All of these factors mean that the peer tutors can often do the matching of child and task more effectively than teachers.

There are clear benefits to a child's learning achieved by the process of teaching someone else as outlined above; there are also clear benefits for the tutee. However there are also clear benefits for the overall learning process in the classroom. We use an analogy from Geography when explaining this to teachers.

We see the teacher as holding the map, or the curriculum; in this sense the teacher's job is to do with the overview of where all the children need to go and what they need to learn. They are concerned with the macro organisation and planning in the classroom. Therefore teachers understandably look for tasks that they can give to thirty children and then they try and adjust the task to accommodate a variety of levels. What the peer tutor can do is to provide the individual focused task at a micro level.

The teacher has the big map with which they can see the direction in which the class is going, but there may be twenty or so different routes through the streets that the children might take, all of which will get to the destination. The tutor child is leading the tutee child by the hand through streets that they know very well; sometimes these are streets that the teacher has never gone through because they had no difficulty in flying to the destination; sometimes they are streets that the teacher only went through once because they learned quickly, and sometimes they are streets they only vaguely recollect because they went through them so long ago. The child tutors are prepared to try out many routes without tiring, because they are only doing it for one person. This is the reason that support teachers are valued so highly: they are able to try things in a variety of ways, because they are only doing this for one person.

If the teacher views things in this way then they can come to a point where they stop criticising themselves for not being able to meet the individual needs of all the children and come to see their own role as one of facilitator and organiser.

The success of Differentiation by Paired Task relates to the type of task, the collaboration involved and the peer tutoring that results. The way in which this can be done is outlined in the structured section below. This should be seen as an incremental approach where children should be introduced to these paired activities in the order outlined as the later paired structures require higher order skills which will be explicitly taught and so develop through earlier structures.

The authors see the peer tutoring as comprising three stages:
- Stage One – peer tutoring on targets set by the teacher.
- Stage Two – peer tutoring on targets set by the peer tutor.
- Stage Three – peer tutoring on targets set by the tutee.

Stage One – peer tutoring on targets set by the teacher

This stage is where children are learning to collaborate for peer tutoring, to give and receive help, on tasks and targets that have been identified by the teacher. In Stage One the teacher provides the criteria for assessment, provides the targets for peer tutoring pairs and assesses the outcome of the tutoring. Then the role of the tutor is mainly one of supporter, praiser and encourager and this builds up the relationship of trust and security.

The teacher may also need to have an input in matching the peer tutoring pairs for a balance of strengths and weaknesses, as outlined in point three. This is best done as a result of children sharing their strengths and weaknesses rather than the teacher's assessment of these, see point four below.

1. Random pairs

The assumption made by the authors is that the teacher will have been using random pairwork, as outlined earlier, for a number of weeks before embarking on this work. This is because this work demands that children have a degree of trust in their pairing. The work cannot be addressed through friendship pairs because this pairing will not have a match of appropriate strengths and weaknesses.

Part of the trust that needs to be built up is for children to know that their efforts will be recognised by their partner and not put down. Since most effective teaching rests upon being able to give specific positive feedback or praise children need to be able to explore the best way to do this.

2. Learning to give feedback

This can be achieved by a whole circle discussion on how to give feedback. The teacher should ask the children how it makes them feel if someone says 'That's rubbish,' about their work, even if they themselves know that their work is not very good.

Children are very open about how bad it makes them feel, even if some cover this with a completely opposite statement like 'I don't care.' The teacher can next draw out from the children that saying things like 'That's rubbish' doesn't help, it just makes people feel bad. The teacher can then establish the fact that the children need an alternative set of words with which to describe work. The children can be asked to contribute to a brainstorm of the sorts of things they could say instead. Children usually come up with phrases which mimic teachers such as:

'That's a really good try but the ending's a bit weak.'
'I really enjoyed this story but I got confused about the characters.'
'You've done that drawing really well so would you like to add some colour to make it stand out more?'

The formula for this effective feedback is to say a positive thing followed by something that they could improve on. It should be emphasised to the children that both these things need to be specific not global. For example they should not be using phrases like 'That's good' or 'That's rubbish.' Clearly teachers need to model this 'being specific' part of effective feedback themselves.

3. Teachers setting targets and selecting pairs

Teachers have two roles to play in enabling target setting to take place. One is modelling the language for the helper to allow the other child to identify for themselves what their difficulty is through open questioning. The other way is by offering a strategy to deal with the problem which involves selecting another child who has a recognised strength in that area and asking them for help and support. This legitimises the process of asking for help from one's peers. An example of this is when a teacher was listening to child who was struggling to read longer words.

T: What words did you find hardest to read?
C: The big words.
T: What is it you found hard with reading the big words?
C: They are too long and I don't know how they sound out.
T: So you want to know how to sound words out better?
C: Yes.

T. S and J in our class are really good at sounding out the long words. Would you like them to work with you and help you when you are reading?

C: Suppose so.

T: Who do you think would be best at helping you?

C: I don't like S, he never plays with me.

T: Do you want to ask J on your own or would you like me to come and ask with you?

The terms and times for specific help with reading can then be established with the teacher or by the children alone. The teacher suggestion gives asking for help a 'seal of approval' which allows children to see 'asking for help' of other children as part of a normal day to day classroom activity . We have found that the process often results in children helping both at appointed reading times and on a more ad hoc basis. We have seen tutoring relationships develop into lasting friendships between unlikely pairings.

Teachers need to beware of blocking pairings because of a history of misbehaviour or previous difficulties in working together. Work with random pairs may have already begun to improve such difficult pairings. Stage One re-establishes children's natural inclination and ability to help their peers which may have been quashed by a competitive environment created by children working individually.

4. Matching strengths and weaknesses

For effective peer tutoring the starting place is a declaration of strengths and weaknesses. This is best achieved by the children talking in pairs about what they feel are their strengths and weaknesses, receiving feedback on the accuracy of their perceptions from their partner. They may then fill in a sheet like the one in Figure 5.4 to help with target setting. This should then be followed by a whole class circle where strengths and weaknesses can be declared so that children are more able to match themselves with someone who can meet their weakness with a strength. This may mean initially that the few children who declare that they are good at speaking or maths are inundated with requests for support and help. Our experience is that children are well able to cope with this, perhaps because of the increase in self-esteem that they seem to experience. Gradually, as more children see how the peer tutoring works, they may feel able to offer a strength. As the learning strategies become part of the conversation in the classroom, more and more children talk about the ways in which they go about learning something and offer it to others as a method to try. This work is called metacognition, that is, the understanding of how we learn, not just what we learn.

I am friends with

I am good at

I am interested in

I would like to

be friends with	be good at	learn about

name .... date ....

Figure 5.4 Identifying strengths and target setting (© Helen Newton).

5. Learning the verbal and non-verbal skills needed for helping others

There are a variety of skills that children need in order to help one another and to teach each other effectively. Some children bring these skills with them to the classroom, some are developed through collaboration and some need to be explicitly taught. These skills include:

- turn taking;
- non-verbal skills such as encouraging with head nods and smiling;
- speaking and listening skills – such as paraphrasing, summarising;
- acknowledging the worth of the other person's contributions;
- including and linking the ideas and contributions of the other person before adding your own.

Once the children have acquired these skills they are able to talk together, listen to other ideas, share out the task and contribute to the product of the task. One effective way of teaching these skills is by organising the children into threes with one person taking the role of observer and using an observation schedule to give feedback on how well they have carried out the skill or skills they have been practising for example: turn taking, listening, linking ideas. The observation schedules in Figures 2.1 and 2.3 can be adopted here.

For more ideas on ways in which these skills can be taught see McNamara and Moreton, 1993.

6. Learning the skills of teaching so you can teach others

The most important teaching skill for the peer tutor to learn is not so much the content as the ability to help. It is very important to develop the children's ability to give help appropriately, so that the person being tutored (the tutee) is helped in the task but learning and independence are also encouraged. We have found that the following five levels of helping are generic and can be taught to tutors who then can apply them to whatever skill they are teaching to their tutee.

1. Demonstrating;
2. Doing it with them;
3. Prompting as they do it;
4. Encouraging and prompting when necessary;
5. Praising.

Five levels of helping

They follow a pattern of doing it for them, gradually withdrawing the level of support to a point of independence. Teachers will recognise this as good practice in teaching but can acknowledge that it is virtually impossible to do this for every single child on every single occasion when it is needed. The following examples put the Five Levels into context.

Example 1. Writing the letter 'a' correctly

1. Demonstrating – the tutor writes the letter several times and uses verbal instruction to themselves, 'Start in the middle, all the way round, up to the top, down the stick and round and flick' with the tutee watching.
2. Doing it with them – the tutor holds the hand of the tutee whilst they write the letter and both say the verbal instruction.
3. Prompting as they do it – tutee holds the pencil alone and both say the verbal instruction and gradually the tutor lowers their voice so the tutee is saying and doing it alone.
4. Encouraging and prompting when necessary – tutee writes alone and tutor says 'Well done, that's right,' and only gives instructional prompts when needed.
5. Praising – tutee writes several letters and the tutor praises their effort and their result, pointing out the correct formation of the letter without referring to any that are not correctly formed.

Example 2. Reading

This example is appropriate for Early Years, Key Stage One and Two. All that changes is the length and complexity of the text being read.

1. Demonstrating – tutor reads aloud to the tutee.
2. Doing it with them – tutor then reads with the tutee.
3. Prompting as they do it – tutor reads with the tutee, gradually lowering their voice so that the tutee takes over.
4. Encouraging and prompting when necessary – tutee reads with the tutor, encouraging tutee to use a word attack strategy when they get stuck, only prompting on unrecognised words.
5. Praising – tutee reads to tutor who regularly praises throughout the text and at the end of the text picks one or two aspects of the reading for specific praise e.g. 'You worked out loads of words using the letter sounds', or 'You used lots of different expressions when it was people talking in the story.'

To help the tutee improve their skills they can be observed by a third person using the observational schedule in Figure 5.5.

This form of help combined with other paired reading activities enables the Key Stage One teacher to provide endless amounts of reading aloud practice. This mitigates against children's difficulties when there is little support from the home in encouraging children to practise reading. The constant practice through peer tutoring should mean that the teacher will no longer feel they need to listen to *every* child read every day or every week. This creates the time for the teacher to give 'quality time' to listening to children read, talking with children about the stories read and giving them a 'reading conference'. The modelling of this quality conferencing about the book that has been read is important for demonstrating how children can target set for their own future reading needs.

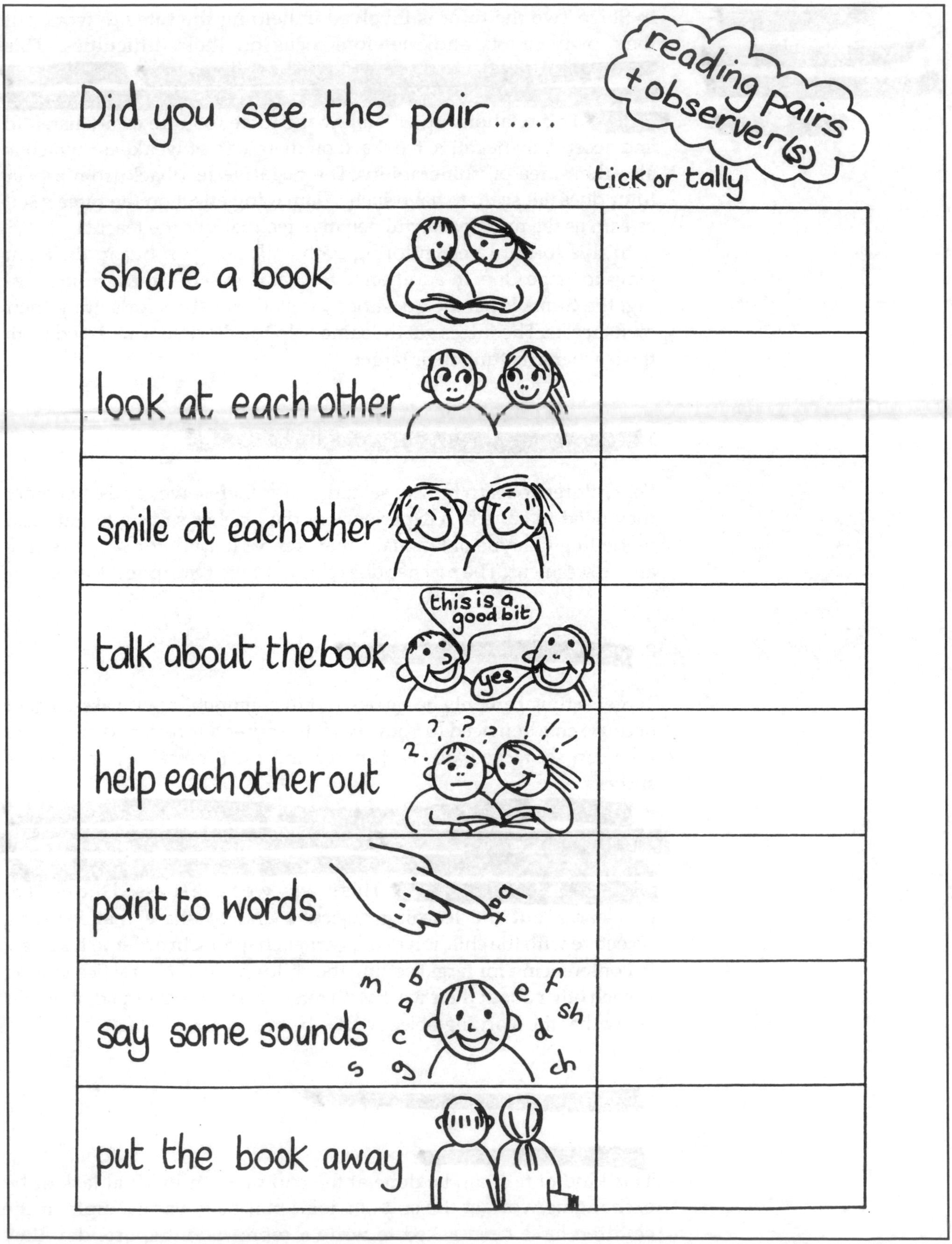

Figure 5.5 Observer's sheet (© Helen Newton).

Stage Two – peer tutoring on targets set by the peer tutor

In Stage Two the tutor is involved in helping the tutee to work out their own targets and therefore focus on their difficulties. This requires the giving of honest feedback as well as praise. This is where the trusting relationship between the tutor and tutee becomes paramount. This relationship will allow the tutee to more easily listen to and accept any negative feedback on their area of weakness which is also their area of vulnerability. The negative feedback from a peer tutor does not seem to have such a damaging effect on the tutee's self esteem as the more powerful negative feedback of the teacher.

In this form of peer tutoring both children gain but in different ways to Stage One. In addition to the gains in self-esteem from helping, the tutors learn the questions to ask themselves for setting their own targets. The tutees get the same help they formerly received from the teacher in setting their targets.

1. Teacher modelling the target setting language

For children to learn how to set targets for themselves and each other they need to have had experience of the teacher setting targets and modelling the type of language that is most helpful for target setting and assessment. The teacher does this in Stage One, point three.

2. Sharing the criteria of success

Target setting can only be carried out in conjunction with assessment because children need to know what the criteria for success are before they can set targets, for each other and for themselves, to achieve success.

Target setting is possible only when the children are quite clear about the criteria for success. For this the teacher must have planned the children's curriculum with these criteria in mind and have shared the criteria with the children. This is why we have stressed the need to be clear about the learning objective and to share that learning objective with the children in our earlier chapters. In order to take part in conferencing for target setting the children need to practice talking to each other about their work with reference to the criteria that would show that the learning objective has been successfully met.

3. Identifying the target for the tutee

a. Talking through in pairs
This kind of talk can be done at the end of an individual task or by exchanging work at the end of a joint pair task. For example, if the children have been asked to write a report about sports day they could show it to their peer tutoring partner for comments and then listen to their feedback.

Figure 5.6 Sheet for tutee to use after pair discussion (© Helen Newton).

	me	evidence	peer tutor
I can sheet Maths Handling Data: Stage 2			
I can complete a tally sheet			
I can complete a bar chart			
I can complete a pie chart			
I can complete a line graph			
I can complete a pictogram			
I can complete a scatter gram			

Figure 5.7 'I can' sheet for maths.

Such an examination may lead to one child identifying the need for:

- better ordering of the events ;
- a clearer use of the names of people involved and what each did.

The other child might identify the need for:

- a good opening sentence;
- a pithy ending.

Within a peer partnership the detailed feedback enables both the children to better understand the next 'small step' towards which they need to be working . Indeed peer tutors can often help their partners to find a way of getting to that 'next step' because they have often just been there themselves. (See Figure 5.6.)

b. Using an 'I can' checklist

Another way that children may be inducted into the target setting process is by using an 'I can' style checklist at the end of a topic, or as part of an end of lesson review to work out the 'breakdown part,' or the improvement part. In this way all children regardless of ability can be working on targets that are to do with improving on Previous Best. An example of an 'I can' sheet is shown in Figure 5.7. In this situation the role of the peer tutor is to ask the one who completed the 'I can' sheet a series of structured questions along the following lines.

Question format to use with 'I can' sheets

Q: What is it about selecting that you find hard?
A: I just can't do it.

Q: What is it that you can't do?

A: I don't know which chart it is.

Q: Well let's make a list of all the possible charts you could use then we can see which ones you might be a bit confused about, shall we?

In this situation the peer tutor may happen to be very good at graphs, the teacher may have organised for the ones who had ticks beside all of the statements to tutor those who didn't or the pair may have been randomly selected and cannot do bar graphs in which case the matching strengths and weaknesses procedure is adopted.

4. Deciding what to do about it

Once the peer has helped their partner to identify the specific problem their role is then to help them decide what to do about it. It may be that they can offer help themselves. They may suggest other strategies which their partner can do alone and which the peer tutor knows to be successful e.g. handwriting – to try 'scribbling' different styles until they find one that is comfortable. They should reassure the other child that if the suggestions are not successful then they will try again and find another way. Alternatively they can suggest another child who is an 'expert' and could be approached for help. This will be based upon the strengths and weaknesses that have been declared.

In the maths example, once there is a tutor who is an 'expert' in graphs he can devise another 'I can' sheet based on the brainstormed list, see Figure 5.8.

This sheet has an extra space for the peer tutor to sign to endorse the success of the tutee based on work that they have done. The space in the first 'I can' sheet for evidence and the spaces in the second sheet for both evidence and endorsement start to provide a bank of data on which the teacher can reliably base teacher assessment. The need for evidence means that the children cannot simply tick all the boxes or put crosses in them.

The children may want a written record of their target even though this is not necessary for the target to work. The teacher can provide a child-friendly target setting record sheet with minimal writing required. This may encourage children to see the importance of the process in the teacher's eyes. Examples of these are shown in Figures 5.9 and 5.10.

As well as being tutored by others to target set children can also be encouraged to target set for themselves. In this situation they may find that a peer tutor partner is helpful for the emotional support needed when reflecting on weaknesses and areas for improvement and growth as some of these may engender feelings of vulnerability

*Stage Three-
peer tutoring
on targets set
by the tutee*

I can sheet for Maths Handling Data
(Local study data)

	me	evidence
I can complete a tally sheet		
I can select the data for my presentation		
I can select a chart for my data		
I can use a chart to predict changes		
I can talk about the graph showed		

I can make my charts even better by:

_____

What I would like to be able to do next is:

_____

The person I will ask is:

_____

Figure 5.8 'I can' sheet for maths, used after brainstorming.

I am _____

My partner is _____

I can write my name with my eyes shut!

_____

I can say the alphabet in _____ minutes

I can sort the alphabet tiles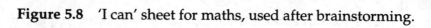

signed _____

Partner _____

Figure 5.9 Child's written records of targets achieved (© Helen Newton).

Date: _____

My name is: _____

I can draw:

spots

stripes

zigzags

loops

I can draw my best friend

I am very clever: Signed: _____

Figure 5.10   Child's record of drawing targets (© Helen Newton).

and depression particularly if the targets are in the same area over and over again.

There are elements of self assessment involved in children setting targets for themselves, and self assessment is vital for independent learning. The peer tutor will in this case be mainly a summariser of what their partner says and feed that information back to them, whilst their partner is working out what target to set themselves. Paraphrasing, which is a form of summarising, is an essential skill here.

> A: I think I need to practice my spellings in story writing.
> B: So you're worried about your spellings?
> A: No I'm not worried about them but I do get some wrong.
> B: You're not worried about your spellings then?
> A: No – it's the length of my stories that really bothers me.
> B: The length?
> A: Yes they are too long really.
> A: So you want to practise writing shorter ones. Is this for the timed story in the SATs?
> B. Yes.
> A: OK. So who do you think can help you? Who do you think writes good short ones?

Once the target is set and a peer tutoring partner for the teaching or helping component is established then the procedure outlined in Stage One comes into play. Figures 5.11 and 5.12 are examples of target setting sheets used with Early Years children when working with partners to set their own targets.

Summary

Through differentiation by paired task and thus the use of peer tutoring the teacher gains about thirty 'in-class support teachers' in addition to the adult support teachers. Peer tutoring also ensures that the adult help is used most effectively. A problem with adult help in our classrooms in the present context is that the help is seen either as a punishment, or as a sign that the child is 'thick', or it is a peaceful haven away from the taunts and jibes of others in the class. Whilst this temporary respite serves a purpose in the short term it does not resolve the basic problem in the classroom in the long term. When peer tutoring is used support teaching will become 'a good thing' and be welcomed by children, not seen as a stigma.

Figure 5.11   Target setting sheet (© Helen Newton).

I know how to write my first name.

I am going to learn to write all my names without copying.

I did it 🙂 well done

date _____

Figure 5.12 Target setting sheet for name writing (© Helen Newton).

Chapter 6

Differentiation by Classroom Organisation

In our model, 'Differentiation by Classroom Organisation' means a set of structures that are designed to organise the children into working with each other and supporting each other. We have specified the structures which we have found to offer a clear focus on helping children to work together.

Most primary teachers use groupwork in their classrooms. Few primary teachers use the structures outlined in this chapter. As many researchers have found (Galton, 1980, and Bennet, 1976), if children are simply told to make groups of four, given a collaborative task and then left to get on with it, they will either be unable to do the task because they fall out with each other or they will get the task done and some members of the group will have contributed very little. The reason why some members contribute very little is that showing what you know in front of a group can be very risky. You risk failing and being made fun of.

The framework below outlines the different types of risk that face children in the classroom. Different tasks create different levels of risk.

1. High ambiguity – low risk; example, complex maths problem in apprenticeship situation.
2. Low ambiguity – high risk; example, small construction toy, only one way to put it together carried out in a group which itself is being watched.
3. High ambiguity – high risk; example, discussion on controversial issue in large group, teacher present.
4. Low ambiguity – low risk; example, simple maths addition, conforms to rules, carried out routinely.

There are some learning situations where the risk is to do with speaking out in front of other people although the task is fairly straightforward e.g. 'yes' or 'no' answers. There are other situations where the task is risky because there is no right answer e.g. discussion or research. Unless teachers are aware of this they can set a task where both the content and the performing of the task carry a high risk,. e.g. role play of an historical situation which requires children to act in front of others whilst dealing with newly acquired factual knowledge. The children have to acquire the confidence and skill to deal with such high risk situations but they need to do so step by step through skills training and confidence building structures.

The structures we recommend in this chapter offer low risk to children in the learning situation whilst enabling the teacher to deliver the same curriculum strand to all the children at the same time. This enables the teacher to have a clear map of the content covered by a whole class while at the same time giving access to the content to all of the children. Through their observations of children the authors recognise that speaking out in front of the whole class is the most risky thing for learners to do when the result could be humiliation. However, participation in a whole class learning experience is one of the most affirming and motivating experiences as it results in personal recognition and affiliation to the class group. This leads to cohesion and a class that is a pleasure to teach.

The structures offer the children the opportunity to practise being in the large group but with very low ambiguity and therefore gain experience and expertise in whole group participation. This will help them to cope with whole group, higher ambiguity situations. Alongside this whole group experience, small group work can give the necessary practice, skill development and confidence for children both to deal with the scary feelings of talking out in front of the whole class and to gain the support and benefits that small groups can provide. The benefits are the same as in pair work, i.e. independence as a learner, support through talk and valuing your achievements, but these benefits can be multiplied in small group work. It is our belief that the pair is the safest place and therefore small group work needs to be built from pairs. This is done in several ways.

Pair work can go some way towards building confidence and reducing risk but it doesn't give any practice in performing in a larger arena. For some children being in a class of thirty is in fact a very high risk activity. The carousel provides the opportunity for the children to work with the whole class in a highly structured and safe manner as they are always in a pair. The children work with many others in the class but only have to work with one partner at any one time. The change of partners is highly structured and offers no risk to their self-esteem.

All children need to have the risk reduced when they are dealing with new knowledge or concepts that challenge their old knowledge. The structure of jigsawing was developed by Eliot Aronson (1978) to reduce the risk involved in research. In this structure children are able to find out information about small parts of a larger subject thus sharing the responsibility whilst finding out new knowledge. The structure still allows all the children to learn and share in the whole subject whilst only being responsible for a smaller part.

Another structure used is snowballing. This is when pairs join into fours and then into eights. This means that the risk involved in children sharing their current ideas and concepts is reduced. The result is that the risk of not getting a correct response is shared among the group. Figure 6.1 summarises three group structures: carousel, jigsaw and snowball.

- **Snowball**   safe because it starts with pairs, information is 'collected' as pairs form a four
- **Jigsaw**   reduce risk, share knowledge and find out knowledge from 'experts'
- **Carousel**   explain and re-tell current understanding, conceptual understanding developed

Figure 6.1   Group structures for learning.

Through these approaches we believe that children can gain access to the curriculum in a way that does not make them feel de-motivated as it gives all children an experience of success as learners and preserves their feelings of self worth. By working this way we have found that it then becomes possible to use traditional differentiation methods such as ability groupings on some occasions without children suffering the labelling, drop in self-esteem and de-motivation which are common results of long term setting of children.

For each of the structures outlined below there is a short discussion of its benefits. It is important that the purpose of the structure is shared with the children as it means the children can work to known criteria and so more easily both recognise and improve their skills.

We also offer a description of how to organise the structure and an example of how it could be used to teach a part of the curriculum. There is a dual intention in giving a curriculum example, one is to illuminate the description, the other is to encourage the teacher to try it out. The examples are, however, just illustrations to allow the teacher and the children to become familiar with using the structure. That familiarity will then help planning. More detailed Curriculum examples are provided in Appendix 2.

Uses and benefits of whole class structures

As indicated in the planning chapter, whole class structures are useful for both starting and finishing lessons.

In our model, whole class work is conducted with the children sitting in a circle, either on chairs or on a mat. Some teachers say that they do not have enough room in their classrooms for this. In this case we suggest that they do this activity in the hall. However we also encourage teachers to consider rearranging their classrooms. There are important reasons for using a circle format rather than a group. Traditionally children in Key Stage One start the morning and afternoon by sitting on the mat, with the teacher sitting on a chair, and sharing their news. In Key Stage Two they start off the day either on a mat or in individual 'places' which limits the flexible use of tables and space in a classroom.

Whole class structures

The problem with this activity is that it seems to create dependency. It gives powerful messages to the children that the only person worth talking to or receiving attention from is the teacher. This reliance on the teacher is compounded when the teacher does 'switchboarding.' A child offers a contribution, another child says that they did not hear/understand and the teacher repeats it. What needs to happen is for the teacher to direct the first speaker to the one who didn't hear. This is difficult in the 'all on the mat' situation as very often the children are talking to each other's backs.

This dependency on the teacher can then carry over into other activities and it is not unusual for the teacher to form the impression that it is the children themselves and their age or personality, which are the reasons for them not taking responsibility for their work or working independently. Such teachers are often reluctant to try these differentiation by organisation strategies for these reasons but are also often pleasantly surprised by the children's latent independence once they get started and 'have a go.'

Organisation of the circle

The children sit in the circle with the teacher at the same level as them and one of the group. It needs to be a circle and not a sausage so that all the children can see each other's eyes. Exercises such as wink murder, bunnies or rain (McNamara and Moreton, 1993) are useful for establishing the importance of 'turn taking' and 'eye contact.' A conch type device can also be passed round for the 'my turn to talk, everyone else to listen' rule to be enforced. The children can be asked to complete the following sentences:

> My favourite food is . . .
> What I like doing best at the weekends is . . .
> My favourite animal is . . .
> If I had a pet it would be . . .

If any children have difficulty thinking of something then give them 'thinking time' and come back to them later. We do not allow 'pass' although if children do not wish to join the circle and insist on sitting out we simply ignore them, but periodically invite them to come in. It is useful to allow the children to take it in turns to be the facilitator of these circle-times, rather than just the teacher doing it. The more that the teacher can praise the children for them praising each other, the more quickly it will be that praise and support become a norm. After doing this exercise a few times the children will get used to it and should be able to go round the circle very quickly. (See Jenny Mosley, 1993, for more circle-time ideas.) The children will already know something about each other through doing the random pair work for both differentiation by classroom organisation and differentiation by paired task. However the circle is a public place, and if the children are to get the benefit of public support and praise for curriculum risks and progress made through target setting they need to get to know one another through the whole circle activities as well.

The children can then be asked to do the 'me bag exercise' where they bring in something from home which says something about them. This means they will be talking a little longer about themselves. Each takes it in turn to say something about their special possession and what it means to them.

To help the children get used to this type of activity we recommend the use of circle-time a little and often. Every day for five minutes with perhaps only five children speaking in one go is much better than one hour session once a week. The content of these initial sessions needs to be social. This is to help the children to get to know one another, to get them used to speaking out in public with something fairly low risk and to give them only one thing to think about – the circle-time activity itself not the curriculum as well.

Once the children have carried out their practices in the way described they will be ready to do whole circle curriculum exercises. Below are four examples of different kinds of circle.

1. Learning circle

The whole class sits in a circle and each child takes it in turn (and in order) to say 'What I learned today was . . .' This can take place after a carousel or a rainbow or a pairs or group activity.

2. Reviewing circle

The uses and benefits of a reviewing circle come from the fact that it is more targeted than the learning circle. It usually takes place after target setting pair work. The children say what they have learned about the topic so far, in relation to the learning objectives, and what their new targets are. Alternatively they may say what they feel are their strengths and weaknesses in relation to the learning objectives. 'I think I am quite good at remembering the dates of when things happened, and the army and battle stuff but I'm not much good at saying what the results and that are.' An example of curriculum content for this kind of circle might be:

> Tudors, learning targets: being familiar with daily life, key military events, inventions and changes to farming patterns, changes in religion, and the effects of all of these on our life today.

To build up to the point where youngsters can participate in this exercise it is usually necessary to introduce a strengths declaration exercise first.

3. Reporting back circle

This can be used following jigsaw, rainbow or snowball and makes the reporting back after these jigsaw groupings both controlled and manageable. It gives the children practice in asking questions which will elicit the type of information that they want to know.

In the organisation of this type of circle it is helpful to use reporting back devices, such as the turn taking devices above. Also to aid questioning, cards with exclamation and question marks can be used. An exclamation mark allows the children to add a contribution whilst the question mark allows them to ask a question. When they have made their contribution or asked their question children must put their card down into the centre and this shows they have used up their turn. This can be modified to use big question marks and little question marks. Big question marks mean that the children are to use open questions such as 'How did they do that then ?', in other words a question that requires the speaker to elaborate on something. Small question marks denote closed questions. These are ones which require a yes or no answer. For example 'Did the Romans wear togas?', answer yes. You could also give out a word card for the open questions such as:

who? what? where? when? how? why?

and children devise questions that use that particular word. For example 'How did the Romans construct their roads? Answer: 'In layers'.

An observer can be used to check to see that the question marks are used properly and that someone in the group thanks and praises the one who has just done the reporting before moving on to someone else.

4. Whole circle – declaration of strengths

Benefits and uses of a whole circle: Children find this difficult at first. This seems to be because of our culture which tends to see all positive thinking about oneself as bragging. The difference between bragging and valuing oneself is that the valuing is based on evidence and is not done at someone else's expense.

Children with low self-esteem may find it impossible to think of anything positive at all, this may include able children as well as those with learning difficulties. Many teachers first came across this difficulty when Records of Achievement were introduced.

Many children with low self-esteem also develop associated behaviour problems which are often to do with defence mechanisms. (See McNamara and Moreton, 1995, *Changing Behaviour*.) Such children may find this activity threatening and may try to disrupt it. In this case 'Compliments Dip in the Bag,' activities (see below, p. 83) are useful.

Organisation: The children are asked to work in pairs first, to rehearse their strengths. This needs to be done initially as a social activity. Encourage them to think of anything they feel they are good at, or quite good at: swimming, dancing, being a good friend, looking out for others, lending pencils, football, reading, helping their parents.

Example: Compliments Dip in the Bag. This is where the children are asked to make a brainstorm list of all the positive things that friends do and the things they think their friends are good at. This list is then made into a series of statements:

> 'This person shares with me,'
> 'This person is helpful,'
> 'This person has a lovely smile,'
> 'This person is good at football.'

These statements are written on cards (the teacher, older children or other adult helpers can write these out and add ones of their own which are similar to those of the children). There can be more than one of the same statement. There need to be at least a hundred cards. All the cards are put in a bag, the bag is passed round the group and the children are asked to take out three cards each. The children take it in turns to read out the cards and then to give the card to someone using the phrase:

> 'I am going to give this card to you Liam because . . .'

This can be introduced to the children by having two or even three circles so that there are fewer children and therefore it takes less time. It should, however, be built up to a whole class activity. With Key Stage One children the teacher or helpers or a more able reader nominated by the card holder can be asked to read the card out for the child. Much emphasis needs to be placed on the fact that this is not a test of reading, it is about giving other people positive information about themselves. One way we explain this is by saying it is about turning the light on inside someone else.

Some teachers are anxious about this activity in case a child gets no cards. We feel that the number of cards helps to reduce this possibility but that also the activity teaches the child the kinds of behaviours which friends and peers value.

The truth of our own experience, that children often 'behave badly' because they do not know how to 'behave well' was borne out by one teacher who attended a training session with us. She reported that after one session of this 'dip in the bag' activity, a boy who was usually in trouble stayed behind after school, collected many pencils which were under drawers on the floor and in other 'lost' places and put them in his drawer. He then set about lending these pencils the next day and begged the teacher to do 'Dip in the Bag' again. This time instead of getting no cards he got several 'shares with me' cards with the card giver saying 'I'm giving this to Ryan because he lent me a pencil today when I didn't have one.'

This exercise helps to change self-esteem because the child can no longer say to themselves 'I am useless'; they are now saying, 'I am useless at most things but some people like me because I share with them by lending them pencils.'

Once the children have played Dip in the Bag a few times, they can be asked to do the Declaration of Strengths for social activities exercise. When they have done this a few times they can be asked to do the Circle Declaration of Strengths in relation to the subject just learned that lesson. Again children need to know what it is they were supposed to be learning in order to do this exercise.

Small group structures

a. Carousel (illustrated in Figure 6.2)

Benefits and uses: It mixes the group without using random pairs. It allows children to repeat and refine their own ideas and to hear several other points of view which allows clarification of that idea.

Organisation: This is where the whole class is organised into two circles one sitting opposite the other. Some teachers may prefer to call this the 'country dance', because of the changing nature of the circles.

This can be most easily set up by organising the children into pairs asking them to call themselves A and B or Teddy and Panda or Batman and Robin, depending on the age of the children, asking all the As or Teddies or Batmen to make a circle with their chairs facing outwards then asking their partners to move their chairs and sit opposite them. This exercise can be carried out equally effectively on the carpet without chairs. The children are asked to take it in turns to speak. For example, all the Teddies speak whilst the Pandas listen. They can then either change over roles with their present partner

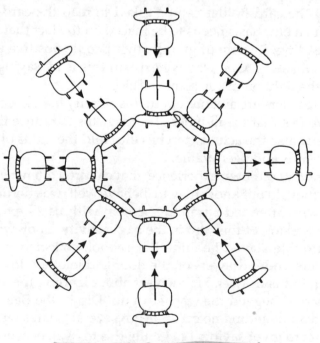

Figure 6.2 Carousel groups.

or change partners first then change roles. They change partners by asking all the As or Teddies or Batmen to stand up and move round in one direction. It is often easier to point to the direction the first few times rather then tell them the clockwise anticlockwise directions until they get used to it . They can be asked to move on one, two, three or four places depending on the degree of mixing you wish to achieve. This is a useful way of creating changed pairs without the random cards structure.

The carousel can be used at the beginning of a lesson to review / recall what we were doing last time, what my learning targets were, what the learning objectives are; or it can be used at the end of a lesson to review learning. If used for the latter purpose the effect of repeating several times the same or similar content is useful for establishing the key points firmly in the mind.

This structure can also be used to share new information along the lines of the jigsaw and rainbow groups. Those who have covered one topic are called As, those who have covered a different topic are called Bs. As are then told to place their chairs in a circle facing outwards whilst Bs sit opposite them, forming an A and B pair.

Example: Geography Key Stage One: Studying a locality
One half of the class, which has been divided into pairs of children, has studied the type of housing. Each pair have recorded on a simple tally sheet the types of housing along the main road and along the smaller roads. In groups of four they have discussed their findings – highest numbers on which roads.

The other half of the class, also working in pairs, has studied the shops and any industry in the same area. They also record this on a simple tally chart and they also discuss their findings in groups of four.

The children form a carousel. The housing half of the class sit on the mat facing outwards. The shops and industry people sit opposite them. They take it in turns to explain to their partners what they have found. Moving them on several times to essentially say the same kinds of things to different people helps to both reinforce their own understanding of their own task, and to hear the other task. Year One children can quite easily be moved on five or six times. They can then be asked to return to their tables with their original partner and together work out a way of recording what they have learned overall; picture, drawing, diagram, writing, collage.

b. Snowball (illustrated in Figure 6.3)

Uses and benefits of snowball: This snowball structure enables children to start in the safe place of the pair and then move on to working in a four to practice the same skills in a group. It also means that speaking and listening skills can be taught and practised in the pair and four before a curriculum content task is introduced, making speaking and listening the task. In an eight the children can work with a larger

Stage 1
Pairs

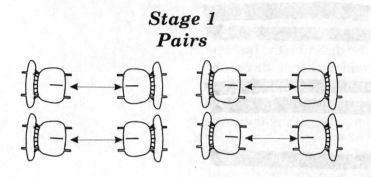

Stage 2
1 pair joins another

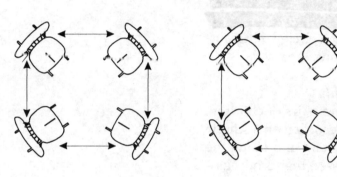

Stage 3
2 fours into 1 eight

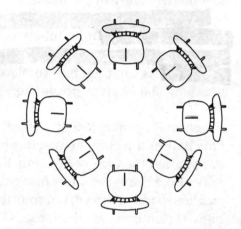

Figure 6.3   Snowball groups.

audience whilst retaining the support of a partner and the familiarity of a small group. It is a structure which allows sharing and therefore the subsequent refining of ideas to an understanding level or even a changing of the conceptual framework, rather than merely transferring a body of knowledge.

Organisation of the snowball: This is where pairs join together to make fours who join together to form eights.

Pairs: To begin the children need to be organised into pairs. For this we recommend a random method. It is important that the teacher explains the reason for wanting the children to work in random pairs and not with their best friend. This can sometimes be helped by videoing the children carrying out a problem solving task such as building a tower from straws and plasticine in groups of five, then playing the video to them. The children themselves can often identify the fact that they are not working together, helping each other, or even listening to all the suggestions made (including some suggestions which would have solved the task). When pressed the children will probably say that the reason they do not work well in a group is that they do not know the others in the group.

The use of random pairs ensures that over time children get to work with all the others in the class for short periods of time, which helps to build positive working relationships and increases the possibilities of partnerships and the formation of peer tutoring pairs.

Fours: In a snowball the random pairs should be joined together into random fours by simply joining two pairs together, rather than forming fours from individuals. The reason for this is to allow the pair to have prepared together their contribution to the larger group and so have rehearsed their input. This has two functions. As described in earlier chapters it is through talking through the idea with another person that the child begins to understand what it is that they think. In addition the pair offer peer support to each other, decreasing the feeling of vulnerability and increasing the willingness to take the risk necessary for learning. Both contribute to increased access to the curriculum. The reason for going into a four rather than remaining as a pair is to provide a small and therefore less risky audience on which to test out your thoughts and ideas. In the same way as working in a pair helps to clarify your ideas, two pairs sharing their ideas allow further clarification. It is through this second clarification that a real understanding takes place, that is the ability to begin to not just know a fact but see its applications. Indeed there is often the generalisation of the way that fact relates to other knowledge and understanding which we have identified as being the point at which there is change in the conceptual framework.

Eights: By combining two fours into larger groups of eight there are similar issues of partner support . It needs to follow considerable practice in pairs to fours to allow children to become familiar with the turn taking maintenance rules of this type of sharing, i.e.

- Each child gives their information in strict rotation around the group.
- The other three children to look at the speaker and give positive nonverbal signals that they are listening.
- No interrupting allowed, questions can only be asked at the end of the child's contribution.
- Time limits set for contributions.
- Signals agreed for the whole class or each group bringing their sharing to an end.

Children can feel very vulnerable in the larger group of eight and it is less risky for them when put into that situation to have recently worked with three of those children, and been closely supported by one. The group of eight is very useful for children to practise expressing their ideas to a larger audience and can also be used for sharing outcomes of research carried out in pairs or fours. This way, for every fact that one pair researches, they get three other facts shared with them by the group. The group is also self maintaining as it follows clear rules of turn taking and children are able to control the behaviour of all of the group members without any difficulty. This then becomes an efficient way of organising knowledge gathering and sharing, whilst practising speaking and listening skills. It also has the benefit of creating more time for practising other necessary skills. In a typical class there will be four groups of eight children each in a small circle sharing their information. The teacher will find visiting these four groups as a non-interrupting observer an ideal way of assessing the overall level of knowledge and understanding of the class by merely eavesdropping on each group. This helps the teacher planning for future learning targets, if used at the beginning or end of a lesson as recommended in some examples given below.

Example: Science: Energy Sources
In pairs: children brainstorm the types of energy that they see used in their everyday life.

In fours: the children use books to research information about each type of energy identified on their two brainstorm sheets.

In eights: each four then presents their research to their partnering four. The eight complete a record of the combined facts about each energy source they have researched.

c. Jigsaw (illustrated in Figure 6.4)

Uses and benefits of jigsaw: This was first designed by Eliot Aronson (1978) when trying to think of activities which would have a high intellectual demand with low risk. This structure is useful for helping the teacher and children deal with the 'body of knowledge' aspect of some subjects, especially history, geography and science. The way it works is for some children to become experts in one aspect of a topic and to instruct the rest of their group in their area of expertise.

Once the children get used to the idea of jigsaw grouping and become proficient in it, it can become a useful way of raising and maintaining self-esteem among children with reading and writing difficulties. The expert is valued for the information they give orally, not for how well they can write. The expert can glean information from the texts or videos, posters, computers and other sources and can listen to the other members of the expert group as they all share their findings and again as they prepare to report back to their home group. They are therefore able to learn from oral reports and pass on information orally. Some children, particularly those with dyslexic tendencies, are often quite strong orally. The children also benefit from the responsibility given to them. They start to develop research skills and become more discerning in the questions they ask when they go to seek out information.

Organisation of the jigsaw groups: The structure is best visualised as a jigsaw puzzle. The children are in groups which each can be seen as a jigsaw puzzle. They are then divided up as if the jigsaw was being dismantled and later put back together to form the complete jigsaw.

There are five or six children in each group. (This will make between five and seven groups in most classrooms). The children are told that this is their 'home group' and that they are all going to help each other

Figure 6.4 Jigsaw groups.

in this group to learn as much as possible. Group mascots relating to the topic can be made to encourage a group bonding. Robert Slavin (1990) who has written extensively about co-operative groups is keen on groups creating their own names and logo for this purpose.

Each child in the home group is then allocated a number, and they are told that everyone will go to join a new group of individuals with the same number in order to become an expert on one aspect of their topic. This new group may be larger than the home group or it may be a similar size. We usually ask the children to divide into pairs to find out about their expert topic, then to come together in the group of six or eight to compare notes and decide on a summary of their expertise before they return to their home groups. They will return to their home group to tell the others who do not know much about this aspect all that they have found out. Once in their home group the children need to be helped to manage the report back. Similar devices to those in the 'eights' structure of snowball can be used, as can observation sheets such as that in Figure 6.5.

Example: History: 1. Tudors
If the children are working on the History topic of the Tudors, groups may be asked to study:
- houses;
- farms and rural life;
- Shakespeare and the theatre;
- dances, songs and court life;
- towns and town life.

during the reign of Queen Elizabeth.

Once each group has gathered information, and they can be asked to do this in a variety of ways: answering questions, taking notes or by drawings, diagrams, keywords, flowcharts, they need to decide how they will order the information to re-tell the home group.

This is where coaching and skills training is needed. Some teachers fear that if the home group has an unreliable child reporting back then

Figure 6.5 Observation sheet (© Helen Newton).

the whole group will miss out on that piece of history. If there are important aspects which you want them all to know this can be covered by giving each expert group key questions to answer. Similarly the home group can be given a worksheet with an amalgamation of questions that cover all the areas of expertise. It is better if the teacher allows members of the expert group to report back what they found before the worksheet is given, otherwise useful bits of information or interesting snippets which caught the imagination of the expert may be lost in the rush to get the worksheet done.

Example: History: 2. Romans
If they are studying Romans children may be asked to look at aspects of the army and expert groups may explore:
- the camps;
- the Roman legions;
- weapons;
- armour;
- siege strategies;
- transport for the army.

c. Rainbow (illustrated in Figure 6.6)

Uses and benefits of rainbow: This structure is similar to jigsaw and to the fours to eights aspect of snowball in that the children tell each other what they have been doing or have found out. It is usually used when the children have been working on different aspects or examples of the same topic or mini-topic rather than when they have studied completely different things; in this respect it differs from the jigsaw group. It is used for a sharing and clarifying of common themes exercise. It provides the same safety as in jigsaw groups.

Organisation of the rainbow groups: The children work in separate groups. These are usually smallish groups of four or five children in each group. Each group is given a different colour – the colours of the rainbow – the children are asked to reform into new groups which have one person of each colour in each group. In this way rainbow groups are formed and there is one representative from each of the smaller groups in each large group. It is usually best to give the children time to prepare themselves, to rehearse what they are going to say before they form the rainbow groups. It is also useful to use the reporting back techniques in the rainbow group to help the children to manage each other in the larger group setting. The observation sheet in Figure 6.5 can also be used.

Example 1: Science: Life Cycles
On each of six different colour cards write the name of a creature e.g. frog, rabbit, butterfly, chicken, lizard, fish. Cut each card into five pieces (each numbered on the back) to produce thirty small bits. Randomly distribute and then ask the children to form creature

4 groups of 6
1 per topic

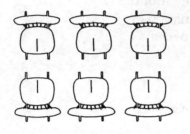

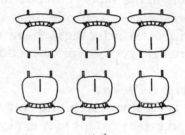

Red

Yellow

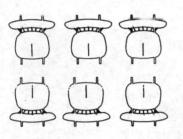

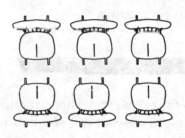

Blue

Green

Reform
i.e. 6 groups of 4 to share what they each found out.

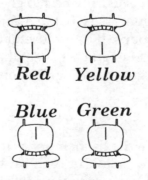

Figure 6.6   Rainbow groups.

groups. Each group then finds out and records in a joint life cycle picture the information about that creatures' life cycle. These can then be displayed. The groups reform by using the number on the back of the cards. These groups now contain a rainbow of colours and a variety of information about life cycles. Each child then explains the displayed life cycle chart their group produced to the rest of the group, who can ask questions. At the end of this sharing each group can be asked to discuss the similarities and differences in the life cycles of these different creatures.

Example 2:. English Reading: Understanding Text using Cloze Procedure
Activity: Follow up to a television programme or other information giving session.

Cloze procedure, i.e. filling in the missing words, is used as a comprehension check for all sorts of lessons. On occasion however it fails to help children to comprehend and it is sometimes completed by children counting the size of the words and filling in those with the correct number of letters. Cloze procedure is much better done orally first and then used as a record of the oral discussion.

Materials and resources: Photocopied worksheets using cloze procedure with missing words at the bottom of the sheet. Large sheets of sugar paper and colouring pencils, felt tip pens or crayons.

- Have enough cloze sheets for one sheet between four children. Use a different cloze sheet for each group, (for a class of thirty this means six cloze sheets). Use six sections of a passage where there is a link between the sections.
- Cut cloze passage worksheet into four strips so that each strip has similar number of missing words. Mark each set on the back with a colour code.
- Provide a 'missing word' sheet for each cloze sheet, again this must be colour coded with a colour to match the cloze it belongs to.
- Mix up the strips from all the sets of four and give out the strips, tell the children to form random groups on the basis of the colour coding on the back of the strip.
- Provide each group with a 'missing word' sheet for their cloze (match the colours).
- Tell each group to use the missing word strip to cut out the individual words.
- The task is for each child to take turns to read aloud the first (and then subsequent sentences) on their sheet to the rest of the group and for the group to try to find the missing word to stick onto each person's strip. Some negotiation might be needed to ensure all the words are complete.
- When all are completed the strips should be assembled and stuck onto a large sheet.
- The children can then be given copies of the filled in sheet so that they have one each and they are then asked to move into a rainbow group, by using the colours on the backs of the original cloze.

- In the rainbow group they are to take it in turns to read out their whole passage, say what their section is about and how hard or difficult it was to do their cloze. As a group they then discuss the ways in which the cloze sheets in the group may be linked to one another.

Example 3: History: Tudors

Here each group is given a different account of the Battle of the Armada – including one from the point of view of:

- the Spanish
- the Queen
- Sir Walter Raleigh
- a cabin boy
- a Plymouth townsperson's.

The children work in groups to consider their own account, this can be on tape as well as written and in some groups the most able reader can read it to the group. The group can be provided with some questions which help them to summarise three key points from this person's point of view. For example the townsperson: loss of trade, possible destruction of buildings, fear for family's safety.

Each group is allocated a different colour, the children are told to reform into rainbow groups and each child in turn is to tell the story from their point of view incorporating the three key points. They can act this out if they wish. The children can then be asked to discuss in their rainbow groups how we decide which is the 'correct' version. This introduces or gives practice for the complex idea of historical interpretation.

d. Fishbowl (illustrated in Figure 6.7)

Uses and benefits of fishbowl: This is a useful way of helping children to work in larger groups. If used alongside fours to eights and rainbow groups it can help provide the practice the children need for working in the larger group as well as being a structure in its own right.

The structure uses pair for support when entering into a larger group activity. It is particularly useful for discussion and for skills training because of the in-built observer role.

Organisation of the fishbowl: The children are organised into pairs and asked to discuss their views on a topic. When the structure is first introduced it is useful to choose a non curriculum related topic such as school uniform. When they have discussed this, after eight or ten minutes for example, they are asked to decide who will be A and who B (or frog and tadpole, chrysalis and butterfly). They need to be told that the As will be going into the middle to discuss the views of the pair and that they will be watched. This gives the children a good preparation for what will follow. The pairs are then asked to brief the As so that they can represent the pair and so they can rehearse.

The As all take their chairs or sit on the carpet to make a circle

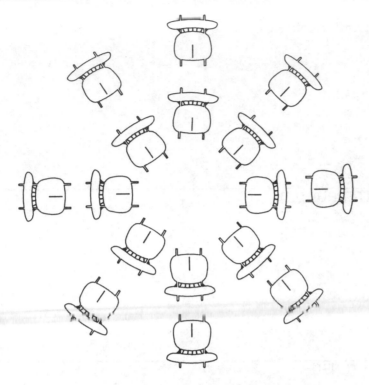

Figure 6.7   Fishbowl groups.

facing each other. The Bs sit on the outside of the circle in a place where they can see their partners but sufficiently far away so as not to interfere with the discussion in the circle.

The Bs are now watching the As like fish in a fishbowl hence the name. The Bs can use an observation schedule like that in Figure 6.8 as well as listening to the discussion. It may be helpful for the class to divide into three groups initially especially if the class is large. For a class of thirty-six for example, three groups of twelve would create three fishbowls with six people on the inside and six on the outside. This could be organised on a day when more adult help was available so the one adult could watch each group or an older age child who has done fishbowl before could be used. For most classes dividing in half so that two groups of sixteen with eight in each fishbowl is probably best for quite some time. Groups with fifteen on the inside to discuss and fifteen on the outside are really too unwieldy except on rare occasions and for specific purposes.

Example: Science Key Stage 2: Physical Processes
Activity: Investigating vibrations – musical instruments
   Materials: Lots of different materials for making musical instruments: pots, beads, rice, balloons, elastic bands, wood, nails etc.
   Organisation: groups, then fishbowl.
   Organise the children into random groups of four.
   • Each group is given a range of equipment and a number of instructional worksheets to make musical instruments e.g. simple shaker, comb and tissue, elastic band guitar, balloon drum.

MEMBERS OF GROUP WHO SPOKE SENSIBLY	FREQUENCY
MEMBERS OF GROUP WHO INTERRUPTED/ MADE SILLY REMARKS	
MEMBERS OF GROUP WHO LISTENED	
MEMBERS OF GROUP WHO KEPT ON TASK	
MEMBERS OF GROUP WHO MADE LITTLE OR NO CONTRIBUTION TO DISCUSSION OR END OF PRODUCT	

Figure 6.8 Observation schedule for fishbowl groups.

- Each group is told to experiment first by making as many different instruments as they like using the instruction sheets and materials.
- The groups are then challenged to make a 'combi-instrument' which uses as many of the experimental instrument processes in the design as possible. The instrument needs to actually work. It can be as simple or complex as the group likes.
- Each group then writes an advert for a music magazine using as many correct key scientific words as possible e.g. vibration. They need to explain in the advert the instrument's:
  - name,
  - what it does,
  - how it works,
  - its advantages.
- Each group is then given a number.
- Groups one and two and three then form a fishbowl, show their instrument to the other groups, the others in the fishbowl can be asked to try the instrument out, play it and make suggestions for improvement. The groups four five and six watch on the outside of the fishbowl and then exchange places so that everyone has a chance to demonstrate their instrument.

Summary

When teachers differentiate in this way they are often surprised at the effectiveness of the structures to organise the children and deliver the curriculum at the same time. They find that the time spent learning the structures is worth it in the end. The increased level of motivation also reduces disaffection and alienation and hence discipline problems are exhibited less often.

The important part to differentiation by classroom organization is selecting the right structure for the purpose of the lesson. This is summarised in the grid, Figure 6.9.

Match Teaching Methods for:

✦ Routines	- whole class
✦ Understanding	- workshops
✦ Conceptual development	- structured, groupwork e.g. jigsaw
✦ Metacognition	- pairs

Figure 6.9 Lesson purposes matched with appropriate structures.

Conclusion

Readers of this book might think that differentiating in this way involves teachers in a great deal of hard work. However, differentiation at present in our classrooms is against a background of competition and differentiation by task adds to this negative atmosphere. The result is children making comparisons in terms of ability and 'name calling'. Research shows that there is a powerful correlation between low self worth and low academic achievement. Our own research reveals children identifying that name calling has a powerful effect on their feelings about themselves and it is clear to us that this aggravates the negative feelings children have about their own ability to achieve, leading to further failure. Skills training for pairwork is particularly helpful in changing this negative atmosphere.

We have found that the use of a combination of structures which allows children to carry out a task in a way which best suits their learning style, whilst being in a situation where they can give and receive help and feedback from one another, enables them to achieve more than previously. Differentiation in the ways outlined in this book increases the child's independence. This means that teachers are able to teach and manage the burden of assessment in an environment which is more positive in nature.

We would urge teachers to:
- believe in their ability to teach the necessary skills;
- use the structures offered in this book;
- believe in the children's ability to work this way;
- allow children to take responsibility for knowing how they learn best;
- enable children to teach and help each other;

and begin today!

Examples of
Differentiation by Outcome

Formation of a river from source to estuary. Learning objective: to illustrate your understanding of the stages in a river's life.

Common stimulus
A video input on stages of a river.

Common task
Children are asked to represent the main stages of a river. They are told that they can work in groups or pairs or alone and that they can use any method or medium to illustrate their understanding.

Variety of recording
Materials can be made available so that children can make 3D card, plasticine, clay, salt dough or paper mache models, 2D paintings or drawings, or a written description. The provision of the variety of materials will lead to a variety of products which the children can present and share with each other. This can give an opportunity for peer assessment as well as reinforcement of the knowledge. The children can be told that they will be given marks for extra details such as oxbow lakes and meanders.

This activity can be used for many other aspects of Physical Geography such as: plate theory, volcanoes, fold mountains, rift valleys, glaciation, sea erosion formations such as spits, arches and stacks.

Living things. Learning objective: to note the different ways in which seeds are grown and developed in fruits, to note similarities and differences between fruits in this respect.

Common stimuli
Variety of fruits.

Common task
Different observational drawings done by the children of up to four fruits of their choosing. The activity in detail: each table of children has a plate of fruit, each fruit cut in half. Each plate has, for example, a half piece of: apple, pear, melon, tomato, orange, grape, kiwi. Each child chooses a fruit

to make an observational drawing and to record the exact way in which the seeds are formed in that fruit.

Variety of recording
Labelled diagram with arrows or numbers or coloured key; write a list of similarities and differences, circling similarities and differences, filling in their own table or chart.

Common outcome
Reporting back on the similarities and differences between the different fruits. Each child then reports back to the whole class the similarities and differences between the fruits for a class recording on the board. This recording system utilised by the teacher could then be discussed with the children to enable them to increase their own range of strategies for recording.

A variation on this same theme is the classification of flowers by leaf pattern, petal pattern and stamen pattern. Each child chooses a different flower and records the differences in their own way . The children then report back on the similarities and differences they found.

The variety of recording could go with any of the other variables e.g. variety of stimuli – common task – variety of recording.

Example 3: History

The Roman Army.

Variety of stimuli
Available in the classroom – books, video material and posters with information about the Roman Army.

Common task
To use the information to make a recruitment drive for the army illustrating what a soldier might expect to get out of it.

Variety of recording
Can include a poster, a letter from one soldier to a friend, a radio broadcast, a video advert, a promotion stall at a careers convention, or a promotional pamphlet.

Example 4: RE

Judaism. Teacher tells original Passover story.

Variety of stimuli
Each group of children given an artefact e.g. seder plate, unleavened bread, skull cap and prayer shawl, bunch of herbs, water and wine, lamb bone, egg. etc.

Common task
Describe the way in which their particular artefact is used in the modern Passover meal and what is its symbolic meaning in the story.

Variety of recording
In a way of their choosing, (oral presentation, poem, writing, drawing, cartoon retelling).

Growing plants and seeds. Learning objective is to find the conditions that affect growth in a green plant and to carry out a fair test.

Common stimuli
Three similar plants.

Variety of tasks
Different experiments. Whole class brainstorms the three different types of experiments. One group sets up three plants with various amounts of water: waterlogged, some water, no water. One sets up plants in compost, clay, and sand as growth mediums and one group sets up plants in full sunlight, partial sunlight and the dark.

Variety of recording
Each child records their plant's progress over a period of time paying attention to leaf colour, number and size of leaves, length of stem and rigidity of stem. Again this may lead to the teacher inputting on variety of ways of recording that are possible and discussing the advantages and drawbacks of each method.

Example 5:
Science

Learning objective: to carry out a local study, present findings using charts and plan an alternative amenity.

Common stimuli
Walk around the streets with a check list of types of housing, types of shops, as a result of class work on things they would expect to see in the streets of their neighbourhood – own chart for own survey, tally chart, pretend they are quantity surveyors in the planning department or architects whose task will be to upgrade the area and plan an amenity that is missing.

Variety of tasks
Come back from the walk, at each table is a different activity to do with using the survey. Represent their findings – in a graph form. Choice of map of the area showing the houses shops etc. Aerial view or pictorially write a street guide pointing out the features of interest and information like shop opening times, chemist openings. Do a model of the planned new amenity. Therefore each child has the opportunity to put together a presentation based on the compilation of as many of the four activities as they have attempted.

Variety of recording
For each work station they can choose their own method.

Example 6:
Geography

Greeks: gods, myths and legends. Learning objective: to be able to retell two stories from the Greek pantheon.

Varied stimuli
Each table has a different Greek myth.
   There can be a single source or a variety of sources e.g. the story retold in two or three different books, posters and pictorial representations of the characters, and a audio or video taped version or their story.

Example 7:
History

Varied task
On each table is a description of the task. One task is to write a short script for a drama telling part of the story, one task is to produce a dressed figure of the god, one task is to make a mask of the god as if for a Greek drama, one task is to design and paint a backdrop for the stage on which a Greek drama might be held.

Varied recording
This can be a verbal recording, find someone else who has done a different story and retell their story using the props and script that they have made.

Example 8: Science

Learning objective: to find out what a magnet does.

Various stimuli
At each work station or table a variety of magnetic stimuli are provided e.g.:
- magnets and other materials such as fabrics, wood, metallic objects;
- magnets of different strengths and paper clips;
- magnets, paper and iron filings;
- floating compass – a bowl of water with a free floating plastic lid onto which is attached a bar magnet, alongside should be other materials such as fabrics, wood, metallic objects, and magnets.

Variety of tasks
The different experiments to do with magnetism that the children are asked to do. They work individually and visit as many or as few workshops as they choose. At each workshop the task is described in detail. Each child performs according to their ability.
- at one table they are asked to find out what things a magnet attracts and what things it does.
- at another they can see how many paper clips a magnet will hold in a line.
- at another they are told to draw the shapes the iron filings make when sprinkled on paper over magnets of various shapes and sizes e.g. horseshoe and bar.
- at another where there is a floating compass they are to work out what makes the compass turn.

Variety of recording
Charts, diagrams, observational drawing, accounts, keywords, oral report. (This can be at the end or during their work at each station to a teacher, peer or other adult asking them to tell them what they have found out).

Examples of Differentiation by Classroom Organisation

Below are just a few examples of ways in which the structures can be used over several lessons to complement each other. They seek to demonstrate how the structures fit into a lesson or series of lessons, offering a variety of organisational methods that promote differentiation. From the examples teachers will be able to see how to put the structures together when planning their own topics and lessons.

Lesson 1

History:
The Romans

The lesson should begin by the teacher sharing the learning objectives with the children which are:
- to tell others what life was like in Roman towns;
- to say what things we have in our lives today which the Romans brought;
- to explain why the Romans came to Britain and why they left;
- to explain the reasons for the strength of their armies and how and why they defeated the Britons.

In random pairs the children take it in turns to interview each other about the word 'Roman'. Children need to be told that one of them is to be the speaker and the other the listener. The listener has to try to remember and summarise what their partner said before having their turn.

In fours the children first share their ideas and then record the joint ideas in a brainstorming activity. The children need to be reminded of the rules for brainstorming. These are that each person has a pen and anyone can write anything. Others in the group can ask for clarification for example 'What do you mean?' They cannot argue, discuss or change anything.

Next the group can order the brainstormed suggestions into categories. These brainstormed sheets should be displayed around the room and the children invited to walk round the room and look at each others'.

The children should then form a circle and ask questions of anyone on anything they do not understand.

Finally children form their original pairs to examine photographs from a photograph pack of a Roman Villa. The children are now asked to talk about the things they notice, things which are the same as today and things which are different.

Lesson 2

The teacher needs to tell the children that this lesson will focus on 'what life was like in the Roman towns.' The teacher should:

- Organise the children into random pairs to share anything that they know about their town in Roman times.
- Ask each pair to offer one suggestion to the whole class.
- Record this on the board.
- Then ask the pairs to see if they can offer any evidence to prove that any of the things written on the board are true. Discuss in pairs, offer evidence to whole class.
- Record this on the board.
- Explain to the children that they are now going to do a jigsaw exercise to explore in more detail the life in Roman towns.
- Have each pair join another two pairs to make groups of six.
- Give each group some books photos or posters about the Romans and ask them to design an emblem for themselves and to give themselves a Roman name. The Asterix books are useful here for raising discussion about the Latin language patterns.
- Tell the groups to decide who will be which number, 1-6 .
- Ask them to reform into six groups of four, each new group sitting in a different part of the room.
- Allocate areas of research to each expert group:
  1. religion, including gods, temples, beliefs, rituals, customs, calendar, place of Christianity;
  2. food, including shopping cooking, meals for rich and poor;
  3. families, including education for children, time and number systems, servants, life for poor people;
  4. transport, including roads and walls;
  5. town layout, including houses, for rich people and poor people;
  6. sport and recreation, including baths.
- Tell each expert group to discuss how they will start to tackle their area of expertise.
- Organise a pairwork review by telling the expert groups to divide into pairs with each person describing to their partner what they will do next lesson.

Lesson 3

Focus in pairs, same pair as for the review. Pairs join expert fours and check out what they are all going to do. Expert groups work on their own areas. Lesson ends with each pair reviewing learning so far.

Key Stage 2. English.
Report writing and
creative writing

Learning objective: to practise report writing and creative writing.

Materials and resources: Several copies of local papers with reports of Bonfire night, poems about bonfires and fireworks, writing, drawing and collage materials.

Organise the children into random pairs to share their news about bonfires. Organise the children into two fishbowls. Tell the children in the middle of the fishbowls that it is their job to ensure that each child contributes their news about bonfire night. After ten minutes the children in the middle of the fishbowl exchange places with those on the outside so that every child has had a chance to contribute, reflect on their own experience and hear everyone else's experiences.

Alternatively this can be done as a whole circle exercise if the children are comfortable with listening to thirty or more contributions. This ability to listen to all the others in the class does improve over the year if they are taught listening skills and given plenty of opportunities to be heard in pairs and groups.

- Organise the children into random groups of four (this is a snowball in reverse: fours then pairs, then fours again).
- Tell the children the learning objectives, which should also be displayed on the wall. Explain that:
  - in their fours one pair is to do the report writing and one the creative writing.
  - they need to be practising to improve and therefore they should be choosing creative or report writing depending on their own targets.
- Remind them of the rule for report writing which is that facts only get reported: details are less important and detailed description not appropriate.
- Point out resource material in the room; newspaper reports of bonfire evenings, poems about bonfires.
- Tell the children to: begin in their group of four to brainstorm all the activities associated with bonfire night on one sheet and all the descriptive words for fireworks on another sheet.
- Tell them to divide into pairs to do the two different tasks.

Task a) One pair to use the first sheet to write an account of what activities their group did on bonfire night.

Task b) The other pair to write a descriptive piece or a poem about the fireworks.

The pairs are then told to:

- exchange their work, read each others' work;
- suggest additions, improvements, check spellings, identify and praise the best parts;
- give back the work to the original writers and the writers carry out revisions;
- after revisions, write up in best presentation style (typed or hand-written);

The two pieces of writing can then be presented on a bonfire collage. The group of four then do a joint drawing or picture to illustrate their work.

Bibliography

Abrahmson, L. Y., Seligman, M. E. P. and Teasdale, J. (1978) 'Learned Help-lessness in Humans: Critique and Reformulation,' *Journal of Abnormal Psychology*, **87**, 49-74.

Aronson, E., Blaney, N., Stephan, C., Sikes, J., and Snapp, M. (1978). *The Jigsaw Classroom*. Beverley Hills, CA: Sage Publications, Inc.

Burns, R. (1982) *Self Concept Development and Education*. London: Holt Rinehart and Winston.

Barnes, D. (1977) *From Communication to Curriculum*. Harmondsworth: Penguin.

Bennett, N. *et al.* (1976) *Teaching Styles and Pupil Progress*. London: Open Books.

Bruner, J. S. (1983) *Child's Talk: Learning to Use Language*. Oxford: Oxford University Press.

Bruner, J. S. (1985) 'Vygotsky: a historical and cultural perspective'. In Wertsh. J. V. (ed.) *Culture, Communication and Cognition: Vygotskian Perspectives*. Cambridge: Cambridge University Press.

Bruner, J. S. (1986) *Actual Minds, Possible Worlds*. London: Harvard University Press.

Blagg, N. (1991) *Can We Teach Intelligence?* London: Lawrence Erlbaum Associates.

Coopersmith, S. (1967) *The Antecedants of Self-Esteem*. San Francisco: Freeman.

Craske, M. L. (1988) 'Learned Helplessness, Self worth, Motivation and Attribution Retraining for Primary school Children,' *British Journal of Educational Psychology*, **58** 152-64.

Egan, G. (1982) *The Skilled Helper*. Montery, Ca.: Brooks/ Cole Publishing Company.

Galton, M., Simon, B., and Croll, P. (1980) *Inside the Primary Classroom*. London: Routledge and Kegan Paul.

Gardner, H. (1993) *The Unschooled Mind. How Children Think and How Schools Should Teach*. London: Fontana.

Gipps, C. (1995) *Beyond Testing: Towards a Theory of Educational Assessment*. London: Falmer Press.

Goodlad, S. and Hurst, B. (1989) *Peer Tutoring: A Guide to Learning by Teaching*. London: Kogan and Page.

Gurney, P. (1988) *Self-Esteem in Children with Special Educational Needs*. London: Routledge.

Hart, S. (1996) *Differentiation*. London: Routledge.

Johnson, D. W. and Johnson, R.T. (1986) *Learning Together and Alone* (2nd edition). Englewood Cliffs, NJ: Prentice Hall.

Lawrence, D. (1988) *Enhancing Self-Esteem in the Classroom*. London: Paul Chapman.

McNamara, S. and Moreton, G. (1993) *Teaching Special Needs*. London: David Fulton.

Mosley, J. (1993) *Turn Your School Around*. Wisbech: LDA.

Purkey, W. (1970) *Self-concept and School Achievement*. New York: Prentice Hall.

Pramling. I. (1988) 'Developing Children's Thinking about their own Learning.' *British Journal of Educational Psychology*. Vol. 58. pt 3, Nov. 88 p. 266–278.

Rogers, C. R. (1961) *On Becoming a Person*. Boston, Massachusetts: Houghton Mifflin.

Skaalvik, E. M. and Hagtvet, K. A. (1990) 'Academic Achievement and Self-Concept. An Analysis of Causal Predominance in a Developmental Perspective,' *Journal of Personality and Social Psychology*, **58**(2), 292-307

Slavin, R. E. (1990) *Cooperative Learning -Theory, Research and Practice*. Englewood Cliffs, NJ: Prentice Hall

Topping, K. (1988) *The Peer Tutoring Handbook*. London: Croom Helm.

Vygotsky, I. S. (1962) *Thought and Language*. Cambridge, MA: MIT Press.